Ordering Our Steps 2:
Focused on Christ

LEO R. SAYLES

CONTENTS

Acknowledgments   vii

Introduction   ix

1   Fix Our Eyes   1

2   Fixed On Christ   4

3   Joy   10

4   Confidence   15

5   Mindset Matters   18

6   Belief: Part 1 – I Believe   22

7   Belief: Part 2 – A Simple Yet Profound Recipe   27

8   The Coaches' Chapter   32

9   In the Stillness   36

10   All In: Part 1   40

11   All In: Part 2 – No Reserves, No Retreats, No Regrets   44

12   All In: Part 3 – Friends   48

13   All In: Part 4 – The Centurion   52

14   A Friend in Need   56

15   "Props" – Our Support Team   60

16   Peyton Manning and the Bereans   64

17 Eulogy – The Art of Blessing Part 1   68

18 Eulogy – The Art of Blessing Part 2   73

19 Cohesion   79

20 Clout   83

21 Miry Clay   87

22 Raising the Bar: Part 1 – Aim Higher   91

23 Raising the Bar: Part 2 – Put on the New   95

24 Maximizing Opportunity: Redeeming the Time   98

25 Be Holy (Set Apart)   101

26 Pressing On: Part 1 – Passion, Poise, Purpose   104

27 Pressing On: Part 2 – The John Stephen Ahkwari Story   108

28 Unity   111

29 Spiritual Markers   115

30 Leave a Mark   118

31 Take the Next Step   122

    About the Author   128

ACKNOWLEDGMENTS

I thank God for blessing me with the gift to connect with people through written and oral communication. God has a plan, and I am diligently seeking to fulfill His plan for me as I share scriptural truths through the lense of sports.

I am grateful for the many coaches who have mentored me and modeled what it means to be a Christian Coach through the years.

I am grateful as well for the pastors who have guided me as they diligently upheld the Bible as God's infallible Word to the churches they shepherd.

Special thank you to my family:

My wife Tanya, for your constant support, wisdom, and advice throughout my ministry.

My brother, Kevin Sayles, for your encouragement and drive as you pursue excellence in your own career. Your passion has helped fuel mine as well!

My brother, Joe Sayles Jr, for your support and expertise in all things internet – marketing ideas, web design and management, etc. I know we learned a lot as we went through the promotion of the first book, but I am grateful for your guidance!

My former students, Ryan Blanck and Gerad Hall, for your contributions in the editing of this second book. Your keen eyes and wisdom were a huge blessing as we entered production phase. It is so meaningful to me to be able to turn to those who were once under my leadership and now are the experts in their fields!

Dr. Zensen, Matt Bollant, Rick Reeves, Deane Webb, Steve McRoberts, my fellow coaches at Grove City College.

Pastors Scott Boerckel, David Saylor, Danny, Andy Frey, you all impacted and influenced my life, worldview, and writing during my time with you.

My advanced crew and "street team" who have all contributed significantly with your support, prayers, suggestions, and endorsements leading up to this publication. Thank you for investing in me and my ministry!

Finally, my daughter Faith Sayles, for overseeing this second project and completing the production process! I could not have done this without you!

INTRODUCTION

Sometime during the writing of my first book I was asked the question, "So, coach, what is your goal, what is your purpose with the book?" I thought I would answer this question as my introduction to Book 2.

Why do I write devotions? My writing is a combination of the gifts God granted me, the training and mentoring He has provided, and the calling He has placed upon me to fulfill His purpose. I have to give you my brief history to see how they fit together.

I was blessed to be a part of a well-educated family. My mother received her Masters' Degree and my father held two Bachelors' Degrees. At the time, I can honestly say I knew of very few African American families at that time who had two parents with college educations (the few I knew are still friends today, thanks to Facebook!). My parents instilled in me a love for reading at a young age, and I was blessed with good writing skills. My junior high school English teacher, Mrs. Hill, loved my writing and encouraged me to consider becoming an English teacher. She encouraged me to sign up for regional accelerated learning programs, allowed me special access to our school library, and fostered my love for reading by allowing me to read literature normally assigned to the next grade level. I received similar praise, quality training and encouragement from my high school teachers as well.

Unfortunately, when I got to college, I realized I could get an A- on most papers without a ton of effort. I took the lazy approach through most of my college career. It was not until my senior year of college that I took my grades seriously and sought to see how far I could push my ability. From my senior project at the University of La Verne to graduate education classes at Central Connecticut State University to seminary classes at Mid-America Baptist Theological Seminary, I was pulled aside by professors who each encouraged me to consider writing educational or Sunday School curriculum.

As I moved into ministry roles, the writing was instrumental in my teaching and preaching. I was blessed to serve under some great teachers with strong writing skills, which helped me further my writing as well. One defining conversation occurred during my tenure as Youth Pastor at Wildwood Baptist Church in the spring of 2004. My senior pastor, Scott Boerckel, was a wonderful mentor for me during my tenure there, and kindly guided me during my final months at the church as I investigated what direction God was taking me. As I was preparing to transition to my career as a college coach, he said something that stuck with me.

As he encouraged me to count the costs of this change in my life, he said, "Leo, there will always be some loss in a transition such as this. There will be areas of your life where you see tremendous gains, and areas of this life that you will not miss. But you will also find that with a change such as this, there is going to be something that you inevitably miss, a loss you can't replace, an itch you can no longer scratch." I wrote the words down after our meeting that day and found them to be true. There were definitely areas of the pastoral ministry that I missed, and one of the biggest holes was that of preaching and teaching. God provided opportunity from time to time as I became a coach, but it was not the same. Nothing compares to preparing 3-4 sermon/lessons each week, plus preparing a Sunday school lesson, preparing for small group teachings, and also for mentoring sessions. It was very easy to delve into God's Word as a pastor because it was expected. I had to rebuild that aspect into my life.

The defining moment occurred when a friend encouraged me to submit a bible-study to the Fellowship of Christian Athletes (FCA) for inclusion in their daily email devotion. The submission was accepted and appeared a few weeks later. I submitted a few times that year, then somehow find a friend in the editor, Jill Lee. She included a discussion with me in an article written for "Sharing the Victory" magazine (Now FCA Magazine). Jill encouraged me to continue writing and allowed me a glimpse into how my writing was reaching people I had never known.

Over time, the devotions for FCA and different speaking opportunities filled a file in our old filing cabinet. My daughter, Faith decided to peruse them and compile a number of them into the first book, *Ordering Our Steps – Committing Life and Sport to Christ*, as her senior writing project in college.

Writing to me is a part of who I am, and also a part of who God has shaped me to be. My writing is an outpouring of the implanted Word of God, which permeates my life. When I consider my writing, the words of Paul to Timothy in 2 Timothy 1:7 come to mind; *"For this reason I remind you to kindle afresh the gift of God which is in you through the laying on of my hands."* (NASB)[1]

I see the world through the lens of scripture; I don't see a great sports moment then try to find a scripture to match it. I see the opposite – sports moments (like life in general) call to memory scriptural truths I have learned. As a teacher, I recognize that contemporary examples often highlight the truths of scripture.

If I can spread God's wonderful love and truth through the avenue of writing, I am thrilled. I love seeing people discover *"what is the length and width, height and depth"* of God's love. ~Ephesians 3:19

My desire in publishing this second book is not to meet the conventional wisdom to "sell more books." My desire is to provide a resource to help guide Christians in the right direction, pointing them toward Christ through scripture.

- I believe this book speaks directly to others with a background in athletics – coaches, athletes, and sport enthusiasts – by using what is familiar in our shared experiences to guide us into a deeper relationship with Christ.
- I believe would be great for:
    o The new Christian who loves sports
    o The young athlete with a desire to grow his/her faith.
    o The college or professional athlete seeking for a resource to help them maintain an active faith.
    o The coach seeking spiritual truths to help them minister to their athletes.
- The book illuminates spiritual truths and hopefully will spark a deeper desire for scripture itself.

If this book encourages you, please share it with someone else. Consider giving the book to a young athlete or coaching friend. Send it to a college athlete or professional athlete in the midst of their season. Give it to a team or use it for a group study.

Be sure to post a review, and let others know if you find the book helpful!

As you dive into this devotional book, my simple prayer is that through your reading, God will help you order your steps!

References

1. Scripture quotation taken from the New American Standard Bible®, Copyright © 2020 by the Lockman Foundation. Used by permission. All rights reserved. www.lockman.org

1.

FIX OUR EYES

Let your eyes look straight ahead;
fix your gaze directly before you.
Give careful thought to the paths for your feet
and be steadfast in all your ways.
Do not turn to the right or the left;
keep your foot from evil.
Proverbs 4:25-28

During my track career, I competed as an intermediate hurdler in high school and a portion of my college career. I translated that training into a successful career as a high school hurdles coach. One concept that was a constant in training and coaching: **your eyes should always focus on the next hurdle in your lane.**

To allow your eyes to settle on the current hurdle you were attacking could alter your posture, impede your follow through, and affect the outcome of your race. From this concept emerged an unstated, obvious key: **Never look back!**

If you clip a hurdle, you must focus solely on adapting your stride and balance to hit the next hurdle in stride. Whatever happens, focus on adjusting to the next hurdle so you can finish the race.

This concept fostered in me and my hurdlers a forward-thinking mindset – an attitude of flexibility and adaptability that has served us well through life. It was a determination that whatever I faced in my present circumstances, I could not replace the past and thus should focus my attention on the future.

This also underscored a great biblical concept. In pastoral counseling training, I recall its importance in helping counselees move beyond their past and embrace their futures. Holding on to grudges, past hurts, and offenses does not allow you to prepare for your future. Neither does complaining about your past, nor lamenting regrets. Instead, the past can foster malice, sorrow, depression, even pride - all with the power to take our eyes off Christ. Jesus challenges us to keep our eyes forward in Luke 9:62, *"But Jesus said to him, 'No one, having put his hand to the plow, and looking back, is fit for the kingdom of God.'"*

As our opening passage encourages us, we must fix our eyes forward, order our steps, and give careful thought to our path. Sure, we are likely to make mistakes, stumble, and possibly fall. God encourages us to get up again and get back in the race.

Romans 8:28 states, *"And we know that all things work together for good to those who love God, to those who are the called according to His purpose."*

If we faithfully follow Christ, He orders our circumstances to place us right where He wants us, in a loving relationship with Him. Let us run our race, with our eyes, *"looking unto Jesus, the author and finisher of our faith, who for the joy that was set before Him endured the cross, despising the shame, and has sat down at the right hand of the throne of God."* ~Hebrews 12:2

Questions

1. Recall a time when you held a grudge or an unforgiven past offense. How did that grudge affect your attitude and/or behavior?
2. Can you recall a time when you forgave someone for an offense or released a personal regret? How did that release affect your attitude and/or behavior?
3. How can today's passage strengthen you to keep your focus on Christ as you continue your journey?

Further reading
Psalms 25:15; Psalms 123:2; Luke 9:57-62

Note

2.

FIXED ON CHRIST

And when Peter had come down out of the boat, he walked on the water to go to Jesus. But when he saw that the wind was boisterous, he was afraid; and beginning to sink he cried out, saying, "Lord, save me!"
Matthew 14:30

One of world-renowned author Corrie Ten Boom's most cited quotes reads, "If you look at the world, you'll be distressed. If you look within, you'll be depressed. But if you look at Christ, you'll be at rest."[1]

Ten Boom's powerful life story testifies to us that in the midst of tribulation, we must keep our eyes fixed on Christ. My friend and fellow Grove City coach Andrew Didonato understands well what Ten Boom's statement means from a coaching standpoint. A 2010 graduate of Grove City, the record-holding former Wolverine quarterback inherited the head coach position in 2016. The previous two seasons, the program went 0-20 prior to his taking the helm. His first season saw no change in the results, which could easily have been disheartening for a young head coach. However, Coach Didonato had his eyes fixed ahead on a much bigger calling than just coaching.

In his first team meeting, Didonato instituted a new philosophy titled "Brick by Brick" and began to instill its three key components - Vision, Process, and Love - immediately.

When I interviewed him recently about his program, Didonato told me,

> "Our vision is 'To glorify God in the pursuit of earning a degree, building lasting relationships, and competing for PAC Championships.' 'Focus on your vision not your circumstance' is our go-to phrase."

This go-to phrase helped his players see beyond their present circumstance and helped change the culture of the program. Didonato continued,

> "September 23, 2017 was the annual Night Game victory that ended the long losing streak. It was a game where we saw everything come together for four quarters for the first time. It was a night when no player, coach, fan, etc. thought about themselves, but rather, everyone came together to support a cause greater than themselves. Hundreds of students charged the field when the game ended and there were fireworks at the conclusion of the game. That night was an embodiment of everything we talk about in this program."

Throughout his tenure, Coach Didonato continued to encourage his athletes to focus on the vision, not the present circumstances, and his team responded. His 2017 team finished the season with a 4-6 record. In 2018 and 2019 his program went 8-3 and 9-2, respectively, with two post-season bowl wins.

The account of Peter walking on water in Matthew 14 is a fitting scriptural example of the phrase "Focus on your vision not your circumstance."

After the feeding of the five thousand, Jesus sent the disciples ahead of Him by boat as He sent the crowd away and spent time in prayer. The disciples encountered rough seas on their journey, *"but the boat by this time was a long way from the land, beaten by the waves, for the wind was against them."* ~ Matthew 14:24 (ESV used here for its translation of the text)

If you have watched popular cable programs like "Deadliest Catch" or other similar shows, you may be able to imagine how dangerous life must have been for these fishermen in Christ's day as they relied on human strength and wind to propel the much smaller boats through the elements. I am sure the disciples' emotions were a mix of anxiety, frustration, and determination as they strained against the forces of nature in the dark of night.

The account continues,

> *"And in the fourth watch of the night he came to them, walking on the sea. But when the disciples saw him walking on the sea, they were terrified, and said, "It is a ghost!" and they cried out in fear. But immediately Jesus spoke to them, saying, "Take heart; it is I. Do not be afraid."*
> ~Matthew 14:25-27 ESV

The reaction of the disciples as He approached the boat cannot be understated – frankly, I would probably scream as they did at the sight of Him walking on the churning sea in the dark of night!

Peter exclaims, *"If it's you, command me to join you!"* ~ Matthew 14:28

With an invitation from Jesus, Peter takes bold action, climbs out of the boat, and walks on the water towards Jesus.

As Peter walked, his senses tried to convince him that his miraculous experience should not be possible. He saw the waves swelling over him. He felt the wind whipping by his garments. His nose likely caught the scent of sea salt from the spray while his feet felt the water beneath. As the earthly elements drew his attention away from Jesus, he feared and began to sink.

As Ten Boom stated, Peter was distressed in the moment. However, he set his eyes on Jesus again and cried, *"Lord, save me!"* ~ Matthew 14:29

It would be easy to think, "Peter, you were already doing the impossible! How did you lose your focus?" However, if I place myself in that moment, I realize I likely would have faced the same crisis of belief in that moment. Scripture says Jesus immediately stretched out His hand to catch Peter, calmed the sea and remarked to Peter, *"You of little faith, why did you doubt?"* ~ Matthew 14:31

The longer I have contemplated this passage, the more I realize Jesus' words were meant not just for Peter but for all of us: If we keep our eye on Christ, we will not waiver in our faith.

Hebrews 12:2 exhorts us to run the race, *"looking unto Jesus, the author and finisher of our faith, who for the joy that was set before Him endured the cross, despising the shame, and has sat down at the right hand of the throne of God."*

The year 2020 taught us many lessons. For Christians, it highlighted our need to focus on our vision and not our circumstances. We are to fix our gaze on Christ, the Author of our faith, who went before us in this earthly existence just as He walked on the water before calling Peter to Him. When the trials and tribulations of life come, we must determine to sustain our focus on Him and not our circumstances. When we do, we find that Christ is not only sufficient, but *"He is also able to save to the uttermost those who*

7

come to God through Him, since He always lives to make intercession for them." ~ Hebrews 7:25

Questions

1. Can you call to memory a "Peter moment" when your circumstances challenged your focus on Christ?
2. How did Christ see you through those challenges?
3. What steps have you taken to sustain your focus on Christ in the future?

Further Reading
Isaiah 41:10; Isaiah 43:1-2;
John 16:33; Hebrews 13:5

Notes

References
*ESV permission in front
1.   Crosswalk.com. "40 Powerful Quotes from Corrie Ten Boom." *crosswalk.com*, 21 May 2015, https://www.crosswalk.com/faith/spiritual-life/inspiring-quotes/40-powerful-quotes-from-corrie-ten-boom.html. Accessed 12 January 2021.

3.

JOY

You will show me the path of life;
In Your presence is fullness of joy;
At Your right hand are pleasures forevermore.
Psalms 16:11

The first weekend of January of 2019, we were given great examples of Christians in both victory and defeat. After winning the 2019 College Football championship, Clemson coach Dabo Swinney was gracious and humble in his press conferences and interviews, acknowledging God's providence and presence in his life and in the team's success. One particular statement went viral that week:

"For me, joy comes from focusing on Jesus, others and yourself. There are so many coaches that are so deserving of a moment like this. To get to do it once, and now to get to do it again, it's a blessing."[1]

Sports enthusiasts witnessed the other end of the spectrum that previous Sunday as well, through the silent testimony of Chicago Bears' placekicker Cody Parkey. At the end of the game with victory hanging on his kick, he faced one of the toughest circumstances a place kicker could ever want; after his game-winning field goal attempt was negated due to a timeout, a Philadelphia Eagle player partially blocked his next attempt, securing the win for the Eagles and ending the Bears season. Despite the horrible turn of events, he displayed great sportsmanship by shaking hands with Philadelphia Eagles players and joining Christian players from both teams in the post-game prayer circle. However, one gesture held the attention of both believers and unbelievers. After the missed attempt, cameras caught him silently pointing to the sky and honoring God. Former NFL receiver Andrew Hawkins tweeted, "After the worst play of his professional career, Bears kicker Cody Parkey points to the sky and still thanks God. We can't just be thankful and honor when times are great!"[2]

Such a strong testimony reminded me of a comment my friend, Grove City Football coach Andrew Didonato often states, "We continue to glorify God by bringing our joy to the process instead of getting our joy from it."

As coaches and athletes, we are challenged to find the strength of character to glorify God in both the good and the bad. During a conversation with a friend who serves as the campus chaplain at my former college, he said to me, "You (as a coach) see the extremes of emotion daily, weekly, each season; the thrill of victory and agony of defeat – yet you have to find a way to keep an even keel in the midst of the highs and lows."

Joy in the Lord should be the cornerstone of what we do. Our joy should drive us as we strive for excellence. But how do we build such joy in our lives?

One of my favorite passages of scripture is John 13-17, the last discourse of Jesus to His disciples. It is fascinating to me that on the night when he would be captured, persecuted, tortured, and crucified, one of His desires was to ensure that His disciples would experience the fullness of joy that comes through a relationship with Him. In John 15:9-11, He said,

> *"As the Father loved Me, I also have loved you; abide in My love. If you keep My commandments, you will abide in My love, just as I have kept My Father's commandments and abide in His love.* **These things I have spoken to**

11

> *you,   that   My   joy   may   remain   in   you,*
> *and that your joy may be full."* (emphasis mine)

He continued in John 16:22-24;

> *"Therefore you now have sorrow; but I will see you again and your heart will rejoice, and your joy no one will take from you. And in that day you will ask Me nothing. Most assuredly, I say to you, whatever you ask the Father in My name He will give you. Until now you have asked nothing in My name.* **Ask, and you will receive, that your joy may be full.***"* (emphasis mine)

Paul, in his letter to the Galatians, proclaims that joy is also a fruit of the Holy Spirit, which we receive as we live out our relationship with Christ. Galatians 5: 22-25 states,

> *"But the fruit of the Spirit is love, **joy,** peace, longsuffering, kindness, goodness, faithfulness, gentleness, self-control. Against such there is no law. And those who are Christ's have crucified the flesh with its passions and desires. If we live in the Spirit, let us also walk in the Spirit."*

We receive the fullness of joy when we are in a right relationship with Christ, daily denying the passions and desires of this world, yet daily abiding in Christ's presence as we fulfill His commands out of love for Him. As our joy increases through our relationship with Him, we are able to serve others in love, compassion, and humility.

On New Year's Day 2019, Jon Gordon retweeted a statement from Dabo Swinney about his chosen word for 2019. I close with his statement:

"Joy, I believe, comes from within. It comes from having the Holy Spirit inside you. We can all have J.O.Y by focusing on Jesus, Others, and then Yourself. This is the perspective God wants us to have daily. Quit worrying about SOMEDAY and find JOY in the journey TODAY. This IS the day that the Lord has made. Let us rejoice and be glad in it."[3]

Questions

1. How might you find the Joy Christ mentioned in the John passage mentioned?
2. How do we attain the fruits of the spirit mentioned in Galatians 5?
3. How do we keep circumstances from stealing our joy in life?

Further Reading

Isaiah 51:1-11; Acts 20:17-24; Romans 15:13

Notes

References

1. Holleran, Andrew. "Cody Parkey Getting Praised For What He Did After Missing Field Goal." *The SPUN*, 7 January 2019, https://thespun.com/nfl/cody-parkey-getting-praised-for-what-he-did-after-missing-field-goal. Accessed 9 January 2019.
2. Relevant Magazine. "Clemson Coach Dabo Swinney After Winning Championship: Joy Comes From Jesus." *Releventmagazine.com*, 8 January 2019.
3. @JonGordon11. "One of my favorite things is asking Dabo what his #oneword is each season. The year Clemson won the National Championship it was love. This is a powerful message about his word this year: JOY." *Twitter* Jan 1, 2019, https://twitter.com/jongordon11/status/1080141064441380864

4.

CONFIDENCE

__Such is the confidence__ we have toward God through Christ. Not that we are adequate in ourselves so as to consider anything as having come from ourselves, but our adequacy is from God.
2 Corinthians 3:4-5
(NASB Translation, emphasis mine)

In Game 3 of the 2018 NBA Finals, The Golden State Warriors' Kevin Durant dramatically silenced the full capacity Cleveland Cavalier home crowd with one shot. With his team up 3 points, 49.8 seconds remaining in the game and 5 seconds on the shot clock, he confidently hit his signature shot – even though every defender on the court, and every warm body in the crowd knew the shot was coming. This one shot was reminiscent of a similar one he made in game 3 of the 2017 finals, with similar results. This clutch moment was part of his record-breaking performance that night which guided the Warriors to a commanding 3-0 lead over the Cavaliers in this best-of-seven series.

When asked about Durant's play and shot, teammate Stephen Curry commented,
"Supreme self-confidence. He works hard at his craft. He's ready for those moments. When you have that belief in yourself, the moment is never too big for you. He would live with the result knowing how much work he's put into it. That's what superstars do."[1]

Every coach desires the "champion" personality on their team, the player who diligently prepares when nobody is around, disciplining his or her body to respond appropriately when the moment counts and honing his or her skills so that the motions become automatic. Such preparation breeds, as Curry commented, "supreme confidence." The Apostle Paul used the analogy of athletic discipline in 1 Corinthians 9:27 when he stated, *"But I discipline my body and bring it into subjection, lest, when I have preached to others, I myself should become disqualified."*

Paul is the perfect example from scripture of a Christian with the confidence Durant displayed. However, Paul's confidence was in Someone much greater than himself. When he wrote his second epistle to the Corinthians, he defended his ministry and reasserted his authority as an apostle of Christ. In chapter 3, we find our verse for the day. Paul asserts his full confidence but does not boast in himself or in his own abilities. Instead, he proclaims that he is adequate, competent because of the Lord. His confidence was so complete, it sustained him throughout his ministry despite many trials, beatings, stoning, and imprisonment. This confidence in Christ was the bedrock undergirding his proclamation from the Roman jail, *"for I have learned in whatever state I am, to be content: I can do all things through Christ who strengthens me."* ~Philippians 4:11, 13

This same confidence is available to each of us in our daily walk. We find it as we find our sufficiency in Christ and learn the meaning of true contentment in the Lord.

Questions

1. As an athlete, have you envisioned making the game-winning shot or stop?
2. How have you prepared yourself for that moment?
3. What steps are you taking in your personal life to build confidence in the Lord?
4. Recall your personal history with the Lord. How has God provided you experiences in your past to nurture your faith and confidence in Him?

Further Reading

1 Corinthians 9:24-27; 2 Corinthians 12:9;
Philippians 4:4-13

Notes

References

*Scripture quotations taken from the (NASB®) New American Standard Bible®, Copyright © 2020 by The Lockman Foundation. Used by permission. All rights reserved. www.lockman.org"

1. Golliver, Ben. "KD's Deja Vu dagger caps the best game of his life." *Sports Illustrated*, 7 June 2018. Accessed 8 June 2018.

5.

MINDSET MATTERS

"Only do not rebel against the Lord, nor fear the people of the land,
for they are our bread; their protection has departed from them, and
the Lord is with us. Do not fear them."
Numbers 14:9

In the modern collegiate sports era, scouting has become the norm in preparation for a match. Teams courteously exchange video in order to study and prepare for the competition ahead.

At times, a coaching staff may find themselves facing an indomitable opponent with many challenges to overcome. Wise coaches must prepare for those difficulties, while also preparing to make the most of opportunities presented. In order to present a positive, confident scouting report to their teams, coaches must approach the process with the proper mindset.

Moses was faced with a similar scenario in Numbers 13-14 with much more serious ramifications than a simple win or loss. Prior to chapter 13, the Israelites had crossed the Red Sea, met with God at Mt. Sinai and were in a restless state, impatiently awaiting the opportunity to enter the Promised Land.

Moses selects a leader from each tribe and commissions them to follow God's command to spy out the land (Numbers 13:17-20). The groups followed their instructions and returned to Israel with their report. Their faulty mindset is easy to see in their assessment of the land:

"We went to the land where you sent us. It truly flows with milk and honey, and this is its fruit. Nevertheless the people who dwell in the land are strong; the cities are fortified and very large;"
~Numbers 13:27-28

When faced with the prospects of the land, this group of spies saw the promise and opportunity. However, their minds were consumed by the hardships and adversity. Because these men forgot their identity as a chosen people and brought a negative perspective to their report, they convinced the nation to rebel against God and not move into the land. Their choice would have severe consequences that would haunt Israel for a generation.

There were two, however, who were able to view the land with a proper perspective. Caleb and Joshua recalled God's mighty hand in delivering them from Egypt, and His miraculous presence in their midst. They recognized the hardships…but they remembered the promise:

"If the Lord delights in us, then He will bring us into this land and give it to us, 'a land which flows with milk and honey.' Only do not rebel against the Lord, nor fear the people of the land…and the Lord is with us. Do not fear them."
~Numbers 14:8-9

These two spies brought a very different report based on the same facts. Theirs was one of promise and dependence upon their God. Because of their faith, they were spared the consequences of missing the Promised Land.

As we prepare for our arenas of competition, we must ask ourselves, are we preparing from a mindset of faith or fear? Will our scouting report reveal overwhelming obstacles or opportunities for innovation?

What will our planning reveal about our identity?

As we seek answers to these introspective questions, our mindset must center on the opportunity for success before us. This mindset should carry into our daily lives as well. We serve a mighty God, who is active in our lives today. Our identity is found in Him. Our road may be difficult, but it is possible… *"for with God, **all things are possible.**"* ~Matthew 19:26 (emphasis mine)

Questions

1. Recall a match against an "undefeatable" opponent. How did you prepare your team for such a match? How did you prepare yourself (and team) to have a victorious mindset for that match?

2. How do you approach challenging situations in life? Do you have an opportunistic mindset or a defeated mindset? What source do you use to prepare to face that situation?

Further Reading

Number 13-14; Matthew 17:14-21
Matthew 19:23-26; Hebrews 11:5-6

Notes

6.

BELIEF: PART 1 -
I BELIEVE

Immediately the father of the child cried out and said with tears,
"Lord, I believe; help my unbelief!"
Mark 9:24

"I believe that we will win! I believe that we will win!"

Through most of the early 2000's, sports fans, athletes, and coaches have encountered this chant. It reverberated during the 2014 World Cup as the unofficial motto for the fan base of the US Men's National Team.

Its origins have been attributed to the US Naval Academy in 1999. Corey Strong, a cheerleader for the Midshipmen, led the cheer with the cadets during their annual Army-Navy game.[1] It has become a motto for teams and fans across the nation and the world.

From a positive standpoint, we know that belief is necessary for success. When retired football coach Lou Holtz was invited to address the Texas Longhorn football team in 2015, he said to them:

> "Every great team believes in themselves. You have no chance to succeed if you don't believe in yourself. If your coach doesn't believe in you, if your teammates don't believe in you, you can succeed if you believe in yourself!"[2]

Belief is the bedrock of success in almost any endeavor. John 1:12 makes it clear that belief is the first essential step to begin a personal journey with Christ; *"But as many as received Him, to them He gave the right to become children of God, to those who believe in His name."*

Today's key verse emerges from one of Christ's miraculous healings found in Mark 9:14-29.

Jesus, Peter, James, and John are returning from the Mount where the three disciples witnessed Christ's transfiguration. As they came into the town, they found the other disciples in the midst of a dispute with scribes, surrounded by a great crowd. One from the crowd had brought his son to the disciples to have a demon cast out, but they were unable to help. In response to a question from Jesus, the man replied in verse 22, *"But if you can do anything, have compassion and help us!"*

Jesus replied, *"If you can believe, all things are possible to him who believes."* ~ Mark 9:23

In his response, Christ turns the father's doubt and despair back to him and lights a spark of hope. The man desperately clutched this invitation from Jesus. He poignantly cries out, *"Lord I believe; help me with my unbelief!"* ~ Mark 9:24

This father's response expresses the dilemma of doubt and hopelessness we all may face in trouble. His love for his son is without question. His desire that his son be healed and his belief in Jesus clashes headlong into the reality of his circumstances:

- The months and years of anguish seeing his son seized by the evil spirits.
- The fire of his hopes smothered repeatedly as he fervently sought help.
- The sheer disappointment he must have felt when even the disciples could not cast out the demonic

spirit.

In this heart-rending moment, we see a glimpse of ourselves as we try to walk between the realms of the physical realities we observe and the spiritual realities we cannot see.

Belief requires us to step into the darkness of the unknown, to trust what we may not see. As coaches and athletes, we have the "classroom" of our playing arena to develop a healthy understanding of belief. We practice belief every season as we set goals and expectations for our team. We practice it as we prepare for a match. Our belief is put to the test as we face an opponent who challenges our abilities to achieve our goals. When we are successful, it validates our belief.

In Christ, our belief does not rest upon ourselves, our abilities, or our work ethic. It relies on the work that Christ has already accomplished, and the power of the Holy Spirit. Our belief – our faith – is a gift from God, according to Ephesians 2:8-10. He then allows us to face trials to improve our faith. Paul eloquently describes the development of this gift of faith in Romans 5:1-5:

"Therefore, having been justified by faith, we have peace with God through our Lord Jesus Christ, through whom also we have access by faith into this grace in which we stand, and rejoice in hope of the glory of God. And not only that, but we also glory in tribulations, knowing that tribulation produces perseverance; and perseverance, character; and character, hope. Now hope does not disappoint, because the love of God has been poured out in our hearts by the Holy Spirit who was given to us."

In today's passage, Jesus led the man to overcome the defects of his faith, before He cast out the demons from the son. The man was right to implore Jesus to increase his faith. As we face trials and tribulations – whether they are the minor trials and challenges we face in our classroom of sport, or the real-life challenges we face in our world today - may we cry to Jesus as well!

Questions

1. Reflect upon a crisis of belief you have faced in athletics. How did you overcome it?
2. Have you faced a crisis of belief in your life?
3. If so, how did God guide you through to a deeper faith?

Further Reading

John 1:12-13; 2 Chronicles 20:1-24

Notes

References

1. Martinelli, Michelle R. "Navy Students started "I Believe that we will win" chant." *USA Today*, 9 November 2017, https://www.usatoday.com/story/sports/ftw/2017/12/09/how-2-naval-academy-students-started-the-famous-i-believe-that-we-will-win-chant/108465568/. Accessed 12 November 2017.
2. Willis, Halston. "Lou Holtz talks to Texas Football about accountability, does magic tricks." *Burnt Orange Nation*, 16 August 2016, https://www.burntorangenation.com/football/2016/8/31/12715556/lou-holtz-texas-longhorns-football-accountability. Accessed 10 12 2020.

7.

BELIEF: PART 2 -
A SIMPLE YET PROFOUND RECIPE

When He had come to His own country, He taught them in their synagogue, so that they were astonished… Now He did not do many mighty works there because of their unbelief.
Matthew 13:54a, 58

In our previous devotion, I shared a popular quote from Lou Holtz, "If your coach doesn't believe in you, if your teammates don't believe in you, you can succeed if you believe in yourself!"[1]

There is much truth in Holtz's statement. The opposite is true as well; **without belief, it is highly unlikely you will be successful.**

Hebrews 11:6 succinctly affirms this concept when the writer states: *"But without faith it is impossible to please Him, for he who comes to God must believe that He is, and that He is a rewarder of those who diligently seek Him."*

Here is a simple recipe regarding belief:
- Your beliefs affect your choices.
- Your choices affect your actions.
- Your actions prove your beliefs.

In Matthew 13, the disciple reports how Jesus was not accepted in His own land. The people's response to His teaching reveals how their experience clouded their vision in verses 54-57:

"Where did this Man get this wisdom and these mighty works? Is this not the carpenter's son? Is not His mother called Mary? And His brothers James, Joses, Simon, and Judas? And His sisters, are they not all with us? Where then did this Man get all these things?" So they were offended at Him."

Their response was in contrast to the father in yesterday's passage. He struggled with his belief. However, his belief was just strong enough that he chose to trust in Jesus in the moment of crisis. In today's passage, the people chose otherwise. Their questioning behavior proved their unbelief; thus, they missed out on the presence and power of Christ in their lives.

During the longest losing stretch of my coaching career, I recall the moment when I realized most of my players had lost faith in me and the program. During a time-out in one critical match, my faithful team captain challenged her teammates as she tried to raise the team morale. As she implored the team to not give up, she exclaimed, "We gotta believe!"

She was right. The team had stopped believing in our vision and our plan. The mounting losses clouded our vision so much that we crumbled when the pressure mounted. We had several golden opportunities to succeed in late season games… but without the belief in ourselves, we were unable to emerge victorious.

As I traced our progression through the season, it also became evident how deep the unbelief ran. The questionable actions of several players revealed their choices behind those actions, which in turn affirmed my captain's point – they lacked belief. I have coached for long enough to know who ultimately must accept responsibility…me. At the time, I could talk all day about what led to that point, the challenges we had to overcome, blah, blah, blah, etc. But those points were irrelevant, except to highlight one glaring fact: even I doubted. I felt the mounting pressure and struggled with the anxiety that comes when the security of my job was in question.

As I emerged from that troubling season, I stepped back from everything and devoted myself to an in-depth study of the book of James during the off-season. Thankfully, the study guided me back to my own core belief, that coaching is a tool God has granted me to impact lives. Scripture helped me to reorder my steps. I found perspective, rekindled my joy, and returned with a new mindset.

James points out several keys in his challenge to the church to live out a life of faith.

1. Choose faith over doubt- *"He who doubts is like a wave of the sea driven and tossed by the wind."* ~ James 1:6b
    The only way to persevere through trials (whether the challenges on the playing field or in life) is to follow the progression of faith.
    See also Romans 5: 1-5
2. Practical application (action) proves your belief – *"But be doers of the word, and not hearers only."* ~ James 1:22.
    We apply our faith when we act upon what we have learned.
3. Put your money where your mouth is – *"But do you want to know, O foolish man, that faith without works is dead?"* ~ James 2:20.
    Our actions are the outward expression of the choices we make, which prove our belief. Our actions speak louder than our words.

Throughout the Gospels, God used ordinary people to

highlight these concepts. Their actions proved their faith to those observing. Christ Himself acknowledged the faith of several followers in observance of their actions.

1. When the friends of a paralytic fervently dug through a roof to lay their friend in front of Him, He acknowledged their faith and healed the man (Matthew 9: 2-8)

2. When the woman with the emission of blood desperately braved the crowd to touch His robe, He acknowledged her faith and healed her (Matthew 9:20-22)

3. When the centurion begged Jesus to come heal his servant, Jesus praised his faith and healed the servant without even going to his house (Matthew 8:5-13)

In each situation, the person made a choice to act upon their belief in Christ. Their faith is a testimony to us as well.

Your beliefs affect your choices. Your choices affect your actions. Your actions prove your beliefs.

May your actions serve as the proving ground for your faith to a world searching for light. May they serve as a platform for your testimony, and an opportunity to make more faithful disciples of Christ.

Questions

1. Yesterday, we wrestled with crises you may have faced in your path. What verses do you know that can help you when you next face a crisis of belief?

Further Reading

Hebrews 11:1-6; Matthew 17:19-20

Notes

References

1. Willis, Halston. "Lou Holtz talks to Texas Football about accountability, does magic tricks." *Burnt Orange Nation*, 16 August 2016, https://www.burntorangenation.com/football/2016/8/31/12715556 /lou-holtz-texas-longhorns-football-accountability. Accessed 10 12 2020.

8.

THE COACHES' CHAPTER

Therefore He says:
"God resists the proud,
But gives grace to the humble."
Therefore submit to God. Resist the devil and he will flee from
you.
James 4:6b-7a

During the spring of 2020, my college coaches Bible study group had a deep, meaningful discussion as we were working through James 4. One of the coaches called this the "Coaches' Chapter." It is a hard-hitting, straightforward challenge from James to live a life of humility.

As Christian coaches, we walk a path with a fine line separating us from the world. It is a tough balancing act, and we can easily find ourselves slipping into an unbalanced perspective. We struggle with the lines between:
- Pursuing excellence and perfectionism.
- Outcomes (wins) versus process.
- Honest talent evaluation versus elitism.

Our pride and ego often cause us to stumble. Challenges in recruiting and competition weigh in our decisions. The weight of our livelihood can warp our good judgement. Conventional insight often does not match biblical wisdom. Pragmatism, convenience, and expediency compete against principles, commitment, and honor.

During my coaching career, I have experienced both the highs and lows of competition. One emotional high was reaching the pinnacle of coaching for volleyball when I became a Division 1 coach. However, that experience led me to my lowest points as a Christian coach, as I unsuccessfully struggled with the issues mentioned above. A personal study of the book of James towards the end of a dark period helped me find my perspective again.

Chapter 4 holds some essential keys for any Christian coach. First, James lists the issues mentioned:

1. Our pride destroys relationships. (James 4:1-2, 6)
2. Pride is a result of worldliness. (James 4:1-5)
3. Our worldly attitude affects our prayer life. (James 4:2-3)
4. When we elevate ourselves over others, we judge sinfully. (James 4:11-12)
5. We are not the masters of our destiny. (James 4:13-15)

James then gives us a list of 10 imperatives to counter this self-centered, egocentric attitude in verses 7-17. It is a great list to help us find balance.

1. Submit to God.
2. Resist the devil.
3. Draw near to God.
4. Cleanse your hands.
5. Purify your hearts.
6. Lament, mourn, and weep.
7. Humble ourselves.
8. Do not speak evil of another.
9. We ought to say "If the Lord wills."
10. Avoid the sin of omission.

If our focus is Christ and we find our joy and satisfaction in Him, then we find balance as He meets the desires of our hearts. When we stumble and find ourselves out of balance, James challenges us to walk through this list with humility.

He encourages us that when we do, the one true Lawgiver – the God of all comfort who has overcome the world - will draw near to us, lift us up, and save us (vs 8, 10, 12). We serve a faithful God, who wants us to live out a life of faith devoted to Him. Let's love God, and as we grow in our love for Him, we can then love others with His *agape* love.

Questions

1. Reflect upon a time when you struggled with pride/ego issues.
2. How do you respond when you recognize issues of pride in your life?
3. How can today's passage strengthen you as you continue to walk this path as an athlete or coach?

Further Reading

Proverbs 16:18; Proverbs 29:23; 1 John 2:15-17

Notes

9.

IN THE STILLNESS

Be still and know that I am God.
Psalm 46:10

Many of us often face "press pause" moments in our lives, when we are forced to step back from our normal busy schedule and assess life. I personally have had several such moments in my life. Most of the time, it was not in a good light. I was a rebellious child growing up. I was also quite the extrovert. In my teen years, my mom determined the best way to discipline me was to separate me from my social life. During a particularly rebellious stage of my junior year in high school, I spent a large portion of a six month period on "restriction," when I was not allowed to do anything beyond required school activities. It was during this same period when I broke my leg after taking a dare during music camp. As a result of the injury, I not only faced restrictions from my mom, I was also forced to endure severe physical consequences as well. Every time my mom eased my restrictions, I would do something else dumb and end up back where I started.

This next comment will date me, but we didn't have video streaming and social media available then. My family did not even own a videotape player at the time. I ended up reading a lot, which led me to investigating my Bible more extensively. Reading scripture eventually led me to fully embrace the faith of my childhood. God worked through many avenues at that time in my life, clearing my life path and giving me direction. My ministry and vocation are a direct result of that trying time.

The outcome in my life is relevant to the fall out from the 2020 Covid crisis, which was caused by no one in particular yet affected us all directly. We all faced a limited lifestyle with restricted social activity because of the circumstances around us. However, as I reflected on the mayhem of that year, I could still see God at work within His people.

Psalm 46 opens with these words:

"God is our refuge and strength,
A very present help in trouble.
Therefore we will not fear,
Even though the earth be removed,
And though the mountains be carried into the midst of the sea;
Though its waters roar and be troubled,
Though the mountains shake with its swelling."

Many believers found solace in this Psalm and other similar passages that point to God in times of trouble. It is important to note this opening passage before we can focus on today's key verse. God is truly our only solace in trying times!

In verse 10, the Psalm reads,
> *"Be still, and know that I am God;*
> *I will be exalted among the nations,*
> *I will be exalted in the earth!"*

I want to encourage you with a few simple concepts from this verse:

1. **Through the circumstances of 2020, God forced the world to "press pause."** For believers, we should take such moments seriously and seek His perspective. I don't know when Christ will return. But I do know this: It is clear that God pressed the

pause button for the world! What will you do the next time such a moment occurs?

2. **Take the time to reset your priorities.** Redeem the time, as Paul declares in Ephesians 5:15. Make the most of your opportunities. As Paul continues in Ephesians 5:17, *"do not be unwise, but understand what the will of the Lord is."*

3. **Focus on your faith.** What is God's will for you? In John 15:4, Christ said that we should **abide** with Him. We do so by learning from Him through scripture, communing with Him through prayer, and engaging within His body, the Church. Be intentional to ensure your relationship with God is the first priority in your life.

4. **Focus on your family.** God's will is for you to love. In John 13:34, Christ commands us to love one another, as He loves us. This starts with our physical family, extends to our church family, and spreads to a world in need of Christ's love. More than at any other time in our lives, we have been given the opportunity to invest in family. Let's be sure we don't allow the busy life to take family away from us again.

5. **Focus on your future.** God's will is that you become more like Him. We grow in our love for Him as we keep His commandments. Be creative in finding ways to sharpen your skills. Don't allow yourselves to settle into a life of Netflix/Hulu/You Tube and social media.

Be still. Spend time with God. Spend time with family. Invest in serving others. Simple lessons for difficult times. Be still.

Questions

1. What lessons did you learn about yourself and your life during 2020?
2. Were you forced to reset any priorities? If so, what were they?
3. How did God use 2020 to continue His work in your life?

Further Reading

Romans 8:31-39; 1 Peter 1

Notes

10.

ALL IN: PART 1

But none of these things move me; nor do I count my life dear to myself, so that I may finish my race with joy, and the ministry which I received from the Lord Jesus, to testify to the gospel of the grace of God.
Acts 20:24

My brothers and I had the privilege of supporting our close cousin, Michael, as he developed during his football career from youth football to a professional athlete. We were like family, and I often was placed in a "big brother" role by his dad. I supported him in competition since he was in middle school, so I was thrilled to see him take his game to Washington State Univ. and earn PAC-10 honors during his college career. He was drafted and played several years of professional football before wrapping up his career.

When we were in college, my cousin always placed my name on his pass list, so I took great pleasure in traveling to support him when I could. One particular game at a desert school in the conference always stands out to me. This school gave the visiting supporters great seats just behind the team. At one point, I watched him make an aggressive move and direct a big hit against the opposing receiver. We celebrated, but noticed he was slow in getting up. We could see his shoulder was slumped under the shoulder pads, and his arm hung limp as he jogged to the sideline. It was obvious he was in a lot of pain. I took the liberty to scramble as close as I could to see if he was ok. I watched as the athletic trainer removed his shoulder pads, had another trainer brace his arm, and then make a firm move against his shoulder. Mike grimaced, checked his arm for range of motion, put on his pads, and went back in the game a couple of plays later.

Post-game, I asked him what actually happened and if he was still in pain. He informed me he had dislocated his shoulder on the tackle and was still in moderate pain…but neither the blow nor the residual pain hurt as much as the trainer resetting his shoulder!

As much as I prided myself on being a fully committed athlete, I could only cringe, realizing I probably would not have gone back in the game. In that moment, I grasped that my cousin was truly "all in," fully committed to his team.

We honor athletes who display total commitment to their team, amazed at stories such as Michael Jordan's phenomenal championship performance despite having the flu. We revere their absolute dedication to their sport.

Pastor Mark Batterson in his book, *Going All In: One Decision Can Change Everything,* stated "When you look back on your life, the greatest moments will be the moments when you went all in." [1]

Paul and the other Apostles understood this deeply. They were willing to go to their death for the cause of Christ. Yet they were simply following the example of Christ Himself, who endured the cross and its humiliation, excruciating pain, and torturous death. He went there because He knew it was the only way that we could be reconciled to God the Father. He prayed for another way in the Garden of Gethsemane, but submitted Himself fully to the plan of His Father.

In Mark 8, Jesus predicts his death to his bewildered disciples. Then He called them to Himself and proclaimed,
"Whoever desires to come after Me, let him deny himself, and

take up his cross, and follow Me. For whoever desires to save his life will lose it, but whoever loses his life for My sake and the gospel's will save it."
~ Mark 8:34-35

Christ calls us to be all in for Him. We often do not grasp how deep that commitment runs. He asks us to lay down our lives for Him, that He may raise us up as His instruments of peace. He calls us to be set apart for His purposes. **The way of the cross is never easy. Yet, it must be our way if we are truly dedicated to Him.**

Let's be "all in"!

Questions

1. Describe an "all in" moment from your sports experience. What was the challenge or obstacle that had to be overcome?
2. What does it look like to be "all in" for Christ in today's society?
3. What personal challenges must you confront and overcome to fully submit to God's plan?

Further Reading

Matthew 10:34-39; 1 Peter 3:13-22

Notes

References

1. Batterson, Mark. *All In: You Are One Decision Away From a Totally Different Life*. Illustrated ed., Nashville, TN, Zondervan, 2013.

11.

ALL IN: PART 2 -
NO RESERVES, NO RETREATS, NO
REGRETS

*Yet indeed I also count all things loss for the excellence of the
knowledge of Christ Jesus my Lord, for whom I have suffered the loss
of all things, and count them as rubbish, that I may gain Christ.*
Philippians 3:8

Philippians 3:7-12 is one of the most quoted passages of the
epistles of Paul. In this passage, Paul proclaims his passion
for Christ above all other concerns. Upon his conversion, he
dedicated his life for this purpose. Through the ages, his
passionate cry has challenged many who seek to become fully
dedicated followers of Christ.

I have a shirt from my 2012 volleyball team with these words
across the back: "No Reserves, No Retreats, No Regrets."
The phrase was chosen by my team leaders as our theme for
the year. One of our seniors first heard it when she attended
a missions conference that year.

The phrase itself is attributed to the life of William Borden[1].
Borden, a wealthy young man, developed a deep burden for
missions during a trip around the world – a gift from his
parents for graduation from high school. The story is told
that upon his return, Borden wrote two words in the back of
his Bible, "**No reserves**."[1]

During his time as a student at Yale University, Borden's
passion ignited a student movement across the campus. His

prayer meeting, which began with one close friend his freshman year, numbered over 1000 of Yale's 1300 students in similar groups by his senior year. That year, he presided over the immense student missions mobilization conference on campus, and established the Yale Hope Mission as he served the widows, orphans, and downtrodden of New Haven. Upon graduation, it is reported that he added two more words to his Bible, "**No retreats**."[1]

Forgoing many lucrative career offers, Borden attended Princeton Seminary in preparation to become a career missionary. His desire was to return to China and minister to the Muslim groups scattered through the country. Upon completing seminary, he set off for China but stopped in Egypt to learn Arabic. Unfortunately, he contracted spinal meningitis while there, and died a month later. The story has it that just prior to his death, Borden added two final words to his Bible, "**No regrets**."[1]

President Teddy Roosevelt, in his speech at the Sorbonne, Paris, stated,

> "It is not the critic who counts: not the man who points out how the strong man stumbles or where the doer of deeds could have done better. The credit belongs to the man who is actually in the arena, whose face is marred by dust and sweat and blood, who strives valiantly, who errs and comes up short again and again, because there is no effort without error or shortcoming, but who knows the great enthusiasms, the great devotions, who spends himself for a worthy cause; who, at the best, knows, in the end, the triumph of high achievement, and who, at the worst, if he fails, at least he fails while daring greatly, so that his place shall never be with those cold and timid souls who knew neither victory nor defeat."[2]

Paul valiantly defended the gospel until his death. Borden passionately lived his brief life sharing his devotion to Christ with those around him. Though he never made it to the international missions field, his willingness to forego a life of ease continues to impact people today. Both followed the example of Christ Himself,

> *"who being in the form of God, did not consider it robbery to be equal with God, but made Himself of no reputation, taking the form of a bondservant, and coming in the likeness of men. And being found in appearance as a man, He humbled Himself and became obedient to the point of death, even the death of the cross."*
> ~ Philippians 2:6-8

Christ gave up His crown to redeem us. He challenges us to follow Him to the cross. Paul was "all in." Borden was "all in." Are you?

Questions

1. Recall a past experience when you were hesitant to respond to a spiritual nudge to take action.
2. What were your reservations?
3. How do you overcome reservations and doubts so that you can fully submit to God's plan for your life?

Further Reading

Luke 14:25-33; Philippians 3:7-16

Notes

References

1. Culbertson, Howard. "William Borden: No Reserves, No Retreats, No Regrets." *Southern Nazarene Homepage*, 2013, http://home.snu.edu/~hculbert/regret.htm. Accessed 12 July 2018.
2. McCarthy, Erin. "Roosevelt's "The Man in the Arena."" *Mental Floss*, 23 April 2015, https://www.mentalfloss.com/article/63389/roosevelts-man-arena. Accessed 7 July 2018.

12.

ALL IN: PART 3 - FRIENDS

When He saw their faith, He said to him, "Man, your sins are forgiven you."
Luke 5:20

Basketball was my first love growing up (until the realization sank in that I did not receive the height gene). I remember fondly the many hours of practice and competition with a great group of friends on the high school freshman and JV teams. Due to my short stature, the only path I had to achieve playing time was to use my speed and my hustle. Coach Hans Schmidt of Carmel High School is often credited with the phrase, **"It takes no talent to hustle**."[1]

I loved drills that required us to go all out, such as loose ball drills. We spent good chunks of practice diving after loose balls and learning how to produce in the midst of chaos. Oftentimes, we would emerge from those practices with "battle scars," leaving skin on the floor from skidding across the surface to retrieve a ball or tip it to a teammate. Those drills taught me the importance of being "all in," for the sake of the team.

Scripture tells us of a group of young men who were "all in" for their friend and in their belief in Christ.

We find this passage in Luke 5, as Jesus was teaching,
"Then behold, men brought on a bed a man who was paralyzed, whom they sought to bring in and lay before

> *Him. And when they could not find how they might bring him in, because of the crowd, they went up on the housetop and let him down with his bed through the tiling into the midst before Jesus."*
> ~Luke 5:18-19

I often wonder what the owner of the home must have felt as these young men opened the roof and lowered their friend to the floor. I often wonder what went through the paralytic's mind as well. Was he frightened, or ashamed? His friends certainly were not. They came boldly, determined that they would not leave without presenting their companion to Christ.

The response of Jesus has always caught my eye:

*"When He saw **their faith,** He said to him, "Man, your sins are forgiven you.""*
~Luke 5:20 (emphasis mine)

The rest of the passage focuses on the challenge issued by the scribes and Pharisees, and Christ's response to them,

> *"Which is easier, to say, 'Your sins are forgiven you,' or to say, 'Rise up and walk'? But that you may know that the Son of Man has power on earth to forgive sins'—He said to the man who was paralyzed, 'I say to you, arise, take up your bed, and go to your house.' Immediately he rose up before them, took up what he had been lying on, and departed to his own house, glorifying God."*
> ~ Luke 5:23-25

In that moment, Christ made it clear through the miraculous healing that He indeed had power to heal AND forgive!

But I am always drawn back to the friends of this young man: their desire to see their friend healed, their determination to do whatever was necessary, and their absolute faith in Jesus. They were truly all in! Their example challenges us in our daily lives as well. We should be "all in" regarding our personal relationship with Christ. However, a deeper question I find is, are we "all in" for the sake of our loved ones? As we grow in our faith, we are called to be more like Christ, who took it upon Himself to endure the cross for us. He was ALL IN for us, and He calls us to love those around us with the same sacrificial "all in" love which He has for us.

"This is My commandment, that you love one another as I have loved you. Greater love has no one than this, than to lay down one's life for his friends. You are My friends if you do whatever I command you."
~John 15:12-14

Questions

1. Recall a time you went "all in" for a teammate in competition. What were the challenges you overcame?
2. Recall a time when you went "all in" for a friend in need. What were the issues and how did you overcome them?
3. Is God placing someone in your life right now who needs a friend to go all in for them?

Further Reading

Galatians 6:2; Philippians 2:1-4; 2 Samuel 23:13-17

Notes

References

1. Gels, James. "Basketball Quotes." *Coaches Clipboard*, 2008, https://www.coachesclipboard.net/Quotes.html. Accessed 20 July 2018.

13.

ALL IN: PART 4 - THE CENTURION

The centurion answered and said, "Lord, I am not worthy that You should come under my roof. But only speak a word, and my servant will be healed."
Matthew 8:8

Although I am not a gambler, I do understand that the phrase "all in" meant to bet 'in a way that risks all your money in a game such as poker."[1] To be "all in" is a slang term defined as "to be fully committed to a task or endeavor; to give or be prepared to give all of one's energy or resources toward something."[2]

In Matthew 8, Jesus encountered a centurion whose faith caused Him to marvel. When Jesus came to Capernaum, the centurion found him and pleaded with Jesus to follow him and heal his servant. When Jesus said he would come, the centurion replied,

> *"Lord, I am not worthy that You should come under my roof. But only speak a word, and my servant will be healed. For I also am a man under authority, having soldiers under me. And I say to this one, 'Go,' and he goes; and to another, 'Come,' and he comes; and to my servant, 'Do this,' and he does it."*
> ~ Matthew 8:8-9

The centurion believed in Christ's authority so deeply, he knew that Jesus only needed to speak a word. His confidence in Christ's power was evident in his response. "I understand authority, for I have a minimal amount myself," he says. I can hear the implication, "But YOU, Jesus, you have authority over life! Just say it, and I KNOW he'll be well!"

The passage continues,

> *"When Jesus heard it,* **He marveled,** *and said to those who followed, 'Assuredly, I say to you, I have not found such great faith, not even in Israel!'*
> *Then Jesus said to the centurion, 'Go your way; and as you have believed, so let it be done for you.' And his servant was healed that same hour."*
>
> ~ Matthew 8:10, 13 (emphasis mine)

When we are "all in" for Christ, we can bring our requests to Christ with confidence. As Hebrews 4:14 -16 says,

> *"Seeing then that we have a great High Priest who has passed through the heavens, Jesus the Son of God, let us hold fast our confession. For we do not have a High Priest who cannot sympathize with our weaknesses, but was in all points tempted as we are, yet without sin. Let us therefore come boldly to the throne of grace, that we may obtain mercy and find grace to help in time of need."*

More than that, we can live each moment in boldness, as Paul proclaims in Romans 1:16-17,

> *"For I am not ashamed of the gospel of Christ, for it is the power of God to salvation for everyone who believes, for the Jew first and also for the Greek. For in it the righteousness of God is revealed from faith to faith; as it is written, 'The just shall live by faith.'"*

Peter challenges us to imitate the faithfulness of the centurion when he declares,

> *"Therefore humble yourselves under the mighty hand of God, that He may exalt you in due time, casting all your care upon Him, for He cares for you."* ~ 1 Peter 5:6-7

Have you cast all upon Christ? Are you "all in?"

Questions

1. Reflect on an experience when your faith was tested, but the result was a clear movement of God in your life.
2. How did you feel afterwards?
3. How did that moment influence you?

Further Reading

Daniel 3:8-30; Acts 4:1-31

Notes

References

1. Cambridge Dictionary. "All In definition." *Cambridge Dictionary*, Cambridge University Press, 2001-2021, https://dictionary.cambridge.org/us/dictionary/english/all-in. Accessed 21 July 2018.
2. Farlex. "The Free Dictionary: I'm All In Idioms." *The Free Dictionary*, Farlex, 2003-2021, https://idioms.thefreedictionary.com/I%27m+all+in#:~:text=m%20all%20in)-,be%20all%20in,cross%2Dcountry%20trip%20next%20week. Accessed 30 December 2020.

14.

A FRIEND IN NEED

Bear one another's burdens, and so fulfill the law of Christ.
Galatians 6:2

There is a saying that reads, "A friend in need is a friend indeed!"

Former NFL quarterbacks Trent Dilfer and Matt Hasselbeck enjoy a special, dynamic friendship. In a February 21, 2019, article written by Joe Rexrode of the *Nashville Tennessean,* Dilfer talked about his journey from NFL player to high school coach, which is summarized below.[1] The friendship with Hasselbeck played an important role throughout his journey.

Their friendship had a rocky start in the 2001 season, when the Seattle Seahawks acquired them both to fill their needs at the QB position. Hasselbeck was brought on board to be the primary quarterback, while Dilfer's role was to serve as his veteran mentor:

Problem was, Hasselbeck couldn't stand Dilfer, who talked often of his faith while pushing Hasselbeck hard in practice. "It was church talk," Hasselbeck said. "I grew up kind of a punk from Boston, taking the train to school every day, and here's this West Coast guy, involved in [Fellowship of Christian Athletes] and stuff like that. I was just very suspicious, like 'You say you're supporting me but you're trying to take my job.' I doubted he was authentic."[1]

That season, Hasselbeck was injured and Dilfer successfully replaced him. However, Dilfer, in turn, suffered a serious injury in 2002, and the roles were reversed again. Ironically, through the traumatic two-year period, these two competitors forged a close friendship that carried them through their injuries and recovery.

Tough times turned to tragedy in March, 2003, when Dilfer's son Trevin got sick. His illness progressed rapidly, and the family was forced to remove him from life-support on April 27, 2003.

At such a time of grief, there are no words anyone can offer. Dilfer admits that he understandably suffered from depression during this dark period.

A phone call from Hasselback and late-night video games began the process of healing for Dilfer. The article goes on to say,

> "Hasselbeck called to talk football. He sensed Dilfer was considering leaving the game. Dilfer told Hasselbeck he had nothing more to give."[1]

Hasselbeck responded by challenging Dilfer as only a true friend can and convinced him to get to training camp.

According to the article, Dilfer was miserable during camp: "I was crying myself to sleep," Dilfer said. "Of course, I really wasn't sleeping. I was just lying in bed, crying. Weeping."[1] Hasselbeck knocked on the door. He had a Sega Genesis video console in his hand. And so began the nightly tradition of Sega NHL '94 marathons between these two. As they recall, some went all the way until practice the next day. Hasselbeck always played until Dilfer was ready to stop.

And this is why Dilfer, on a "Monday Night Football" broadcast in 2012, credited Hasselbeck with saving his life. "You've got to put this into context: This was Matt's first chance and his last chance," Dilfer said of Hasselbeck proving himself as an NFL starter. "His chance to be the dude. He should be getting rest. He should be watching film. He should be integrating with his teammates. I can think of 100 things he should be doing besides what he ends up doing."[1]

Friendships are forged through shared experiences and passions. The bond of true friendship can fuse so deeply, it is closer than that of brotherhood. Proverbs 18:24 reads, "*A man of too many friends may come to ruin, but there is a friend who sticks closer than a brother.*"

True friends are proven when trials of life face us, when we are in our deepest pits of despair. It is in those moments that the law of Christ is fulfilled. Today's scripture is a challenge; we are indeed our brother's keeper. As we struggle through life, we are to help each other. Life is not a competition, it is a journey. Likewise, Christ wants us all to reach the end of the journey together, celebrating with Him at the Great Wedding Feast of heaven. The term "fulfill" in this passage suggests that helping each other is exactly what Christ expects of believers. By doing so, we fulfill the two great commandments to love God and love our neighbors. We in turn fulfill Christ's command in John 15 to love one another. Let's run this race together, let's finish strong!

Questions

1. Hasselbeck recognized that talking wasn't the right means of comfort for Dilfer. How can you determine the best means for helping your friend through a trial?

2. Do you have a *friend who sticks closer than a brother*? What experience/passion helped forge that friendship?

Further Reading
1 Samuel 20

Notes

References

1. Rexrode, Joe, *Trent Dilfer's journey, from Super Bowl to tragedy to Nashville high school coach* by The Tennessean Online, Feb 22, 2019, https://www.tennessean.com/story/sports/high-school/2019/02/21/trent-dilfer-matt-tim-hasselbeck-lipscomb-academy/2784091002/. Used by permission

15.

"PROPS" -
OUR SUPPORT TEAM

But Moses' hands became heavy; so they took a stone and put it under him, and he sat on it. And Aaron and Hur supported his hands, one on one side, and the other on the other side; and his hands were steady until the going down of the sun.
Exodus 17:12

We all need a support system. Great leaders invest in a system of support because they know they cannot "go it alone." Great coaches develop a system of support through their assistant coaches and team leaders who are capable of upholding their work as head coaches, in essence raising the banner on behalf of him or her.

During an interview for the "Fast Leader" podcast, noted author and leadership coach Douglas Gerber stated, "It's the team that will make the leader successful."[1]

I've been blessed to serve in some outstanding athletic departments and to work alongside and underneath some great coaches. As I reflect on the many success stories found in these programs, one readily identifiable constant was the support network that undergirded these leaders.

30 years ago I developed a special relationship with an exceptional coach in my first position out of college. We worked at a small Christian school and supported each other during a brief 3-year period, often assisting each other in our key sports. Together we experienced a tremendous level of

success during our tenure. Although our relationship started a little rocky – we were two young, proud coaches with very different coaching styles at the time – our shared passion for coaching, love for Christ, love for our athletes, and loyalty to each other forged a bond that has kept us close 30 years later although we live 2000 miles apart.

In the summer of 2020 this friend was stricken with a serious case of the coronavirus. His wife reached out to me to form a special prayer network when he took a turn for the worse and was placed in ICU. Through social media, our friends and many former athletes rallied around him through prayer and messages of encouragement as he fought his way through his storm (thankfully, God carried him through and returned him to health). I sent my friend a brief video as well that was based on today's passage.

In Exodus 17:8-15, the Amalekites attack Israel while they are in the wilderness. Moses sends Joshua out to lead the Israelites on the battlefield while he takes the rod of God and proceeds to the top of a hill overlooking the battle, raising the rod high as a banner of God's promise. Whenever he held it high, Israel would prevail in the battle. However, scripture says when his hands became heavy and he lowered the staff, the Amalekites would prevail. Consequently, Aaron and Hur gave Moses a rock to sit on, while they each supported his upraised arms until the sun set and Joshua led the Israelites to victory.

2020 was an incredibly challenging year for our world. Although sports at first appeared to be a petty afterthought to the incredible needs of the time, the need for sports as one of several critical avenues to guide young people has become unmistakable. The challenges and pitfalls we experienced illustrated to us that we all have a need for a quality support network as well. During my own personal struggle with the virus, I was forced to rely on my own support network and was profoundly blessed by their care.

Galatians 6:2 states, *"Bear one another's burdens, and so fulfill the law of Christ."*

One way God orders our steps is by placing people in our lives who will support us in our time of need – just as we are placed in others' lives to do the same. How are you doing? Are you, (or someone you know) struggling to carry a burden alone? Have you invested in developing a network of mutual support to carry you through the next calamity? If we have, then we will arise above the fray when trouble comes and carry high the banner of Christ!

Questions

1. What individuals in your life would you place in your personal support network and why?
2. Whom has God placed in your life in order for you to be their support network?
3. How can you invest in these relationships in order to strengthen these networks?

Further Reading

Ecclesiastes 4:9-12; Galatians 6:1-9; 1 Peter 3:8-9

Notes

References

1. https://www.fastleader.net/douglasgerber/ May 1, 2019

16.

PEYTON MANNING AND THE BEREANS

They received the word with all readiness, and searched the Scriptures daily to find out whether these things were so.
Acts 17:11

Future Hall of Fame QB Peyton Manning was arguably the best quarterback of his generation. Known for his combination of hard work, leadership, sacrifice and his gentle, unassuming spirit, he emerged at a time when the NFL needed a new star.

In one 2011 article, the writer stated,
> "Few prepare more thoroughly than Manning, and even fewer can match the feats of the league's only four-time MVP.
> 'It takes you absolutely forever to watch one game with their defense because they have so many different players and formations. It's a full-time cram session,' Manning said. 'It just takes you time if you are going to truly study.'"[1]

Throughout Manning's career, his fastidious preparation and video study was featured in studio shows and parodied by comics (even Manning himself). Yet for all of the jokes, football experts understood one important point: Manning had a passionate, deep grasp of the game, and took it upon himself to prepare and plan to be ready for any eventuality.

Manning developed a depth of understanding of the game of

football because of his dedication and diligence to study. While some may call his behavior obsessive, it also serves as a great example of what it means to know the playbook inside and out.

In our current generation, we have seen a rise in the level of "spiritually minded" people who claim Christianity yet lack any understanding of God's Word. Instead of delving into scripture and relying on the guidance of the Holy Spirit for themselves, they too often turn to popular podcasts, self-help books, and popular social media for their daily scripture. We miss the point that God gave us scripture for us to know Him personally. Instead, we bring the "pop culture" into the church.

The Bereans are a great scriptural example for us to follow. In Acts 17, Paul and Silas were discharged to Berea to preach in the synagogue. Luke described these Jews as *"fair-minded…in that they received the word in all readiness and searched the scriptures daily whether these things were so."* ~ Acts 17:11

Because they personally sought to understand scripture and delved deeply to discern if the apostles preached truth, Luke declared *"Therefore many of them believed and also not a few of the Greeks, prominent women as well as men."* ~ Acts 17:12

In Romans 12:2, Paul challenges believers not to conform to the world, but instead to be *"transformed by the renewing of your mind, that you may prove what is that good and acceptable and perfect will of God."*

We all should follow Peyton's example in our study of God's word. We should pray for Christ to increase our passion for scripture. Let others say of us that we are fair-minded and search the scriptures for ourselves.

Then we:

"being rooted and grounded in love, (will) be able to comprehend with all the saints what is the width and length and depth and height— to know the love of Christ which passes knowledge; that you may be filled with all the fullness of God."
~ Ephesians 3:17b, 18-19

Questions

1. If you play or coach a team sport, how did you learn to execute your team's playbook?
2. On a scale of 1-10, with 1 being low and 10 being high, rate your current level of daily bible-reading. Why did you choose the rating you gave yourself?
3. What lessons can we learn and apply from the Berean church?

Further Reading

2 Peter 3:14-18; 2 Timothy 3:10-17

Notes

References

1. Marot, Michael, Manning A Study in Diligence; QB's preparation has Jets troubled. Boston.com/sports.January 8, 2011.
http://archive.boston.com/sports/football/articles/2011/01/08/man ning_a_study_in_diligence/

17.

EULOGY – THE ART OF BLESSING PART 1

Let no corrupt word proceed out of your mouth, but what is good for necessary edification, that it may impart grace to the hearers.
Ephesians 4:29

In a March 29, 2020 Axios article, Ursula Perano reviews a CNN interview from that day with Senator Amy Klobuchar. Klobuchar, whose husband tested positive for the coronavirus said that the hardest part of her experience is that "it is such a lonely disease."[1]

She went on to say,

> "You can't see your loved one. You can't hold their hand. You can't give a hug to their health care providers, who are there all day. All you can do is talk to them on the phone."[1]

Klobuchar's comments echo numerous testimonies from health-care providers and illustrate the powerful images of nurses and doctors caring for patients isolated and on ventilators.

I believe her comments echo a much deeper concern: It is absolutely true that patients are forced to suffer alone without the physical presence of loved ones. The importance of such support has been documented for years. However, the loneliness is felt at every level:
- By the loved one who cannot be there.
- By the health care professionals who deeply desire

to give the best care that they can.
- By individuals left to shelter at home alone, cut off from society: whether they are a senior citizen, or a 20-something alone in an apartment complex.

One truth that coronavirus has revealed is just how interdependent we truly are.

Another truth it revealed is how much this world needs to know the personal love of Christ and to feel His presence in their lives.

Now, more than ever, the body of Christ needs to understand the power of our words. We need to be about our mission, to convey the Good News that Christ has overcome the world. As Romans 10:15 proclaims, *"How beautiful are the feet of those who preach the Gospel of peace, Who bring glad tidings of good things!"*

As we continue to recover from the 2020 stigma of physical contact, we must embrace the importance and power of our words. James challenges all believers in James 3:10, *"out of the same mouth proceed blessing and cursing. My brethren, these things ought not to be so."*

Paul echoes this challenge in today's opening passage.

Dr. Jeff Myers, a friend from my tenure at Bryan College, calls the challenge in verse 29 "the art of blessing." I want to consider this art, and how we can live it out as disciple-makers.

At the time I originally published this in blog form, I received a beautiful example of this "art of blessing" in an email from one of my 2020 graduates.

Here is a glimpse of what she shared:

"I don't know if this is strange for me to send to you or not, but for some reason I am just really feeling prompted to send it to you... I was writing this evening about my return back to volleyball after my brain surgeries and as I wrote I found myself very grateful for the way you handled the situation even as a brand new coach. I copied the paragraph below. As I wrote it, I realized what a perfect picture of grace and truth it was. I just figured that each of us could use some encouragement in this crazy time and figured I would send it your way.

"Heading into our first day of spring practice, I was beyond excited. However, as soon as we got started, I realized just how much catching up my body still had to do. It felt as though I had lost all muscle memory. My legs weren't shuffling to the ball, I wasn't angling my platform correctly, and I was just straight up slow. I was so beyond frustrated at the end of practice when my brand new coach, Coach Sayles, came up to me. He asked me if I was frustrated, knowing full well that I was far beyond frustrated. He then said to me, "I'm not frustrated with you, so you have no reason to be frustrated with yourself. You need to learn to have as much patience with yourself as you have persistence." I stood there, stunned and unable to find a comeback to something I knew was true. I've never forgotten that. I still use that saying going into challenges in my life. I have begun to have patience with myself because of this."

My player's encouraging email blessed me tremendously. Her reflections built me up as a coach and affirmed my personal mission and vision. She spoke grace into my life.

Today, let's all do the same. Let's be intentional to speak grace into the lives of those around us.

How?
1. Ask for God to give you eyes to see who needs a word of affirmation today.
2. Ask for wisdom to determine what to share.
3. Ask for boldness.
4. Make it real.
    a. Keep it short and specific.
    b. A word of gratitude, a memory you have, appreciation for a quality you see in the person.
    c. Be personal.

Let's be the Church at work as we build up our brothers and sisters in Christ!

Questions

1. Do you recall a time when you were the recipient of a blessing?
2. How did that blessing affect you?
3. Who is God providing you an opportunity to bless?

Further Reading
James 1:19-20, 26; James 3:1-18

Notes

References
1. Ursula Perano, "Klobuchar on coronavirus: "The hardest thing is this is such a lonely disease," Axios March 29, 2020. https://www.axios.com/klobuchar-husband-coronavirus-4fe0ddcd-3f91-4ba3-8f33-7165458f08df.html

18.

EULOGY - THE ART OF BLESSING PART 2

Let no corrupt word proceed out of your mouth, but what is good for necessary edification, that it may impart grace to the hearers.
Ephesians 4:29

In the previous devotion, I shared highlights of an email I received from a former player. It was a great example of what it means to "bless" another person. Today, let's dig a little deeper into this "art of blessing."

In 2020 most of us were unable to fully utilize the power of our presence in the lives of those around us. Hopefully, the experience taught us that we have tremendous opportunity to bless through the spoken and written word. My player's email blessed me tremendously through her affirmation and encouragement. It is the perfect example of what we call a eulogy.

Have you ever considered the purpose for a eulogy at a funeral? It is a speech praising someone who has passed away, yet it has no benefit to that actual individual. It is designed to help the family and friends left behind. I introduced the phrase, "art of blessing" in the last devotion, which was first coined by Dr. Jeff Myers. I can recall the particular lunch conversation years ago when he introduced it to me. We were discussing a new direction I was sensing at the time, as I was learning to embrace writing and speaking opportunities to further my personal platform in disciple-making.

Dr. Myers gave me a copy of his book, *Handoff* (a great short read on how to disciple and mentor effectively). He shared an extract from his chapter, which discussed the term "eulogy," and posed a question that has motivated and guided me since:

"Wouldn't it serve a greater purpose to eulogize a person while alive?"

Consider what it would look like if we practiced this concept with each other. Study for a moment the definition and true function of the word, "eulogy."

Dictionary.com defines the word as,
1. "a speech or writing in praise of a person or thing, especially a set oration in honor of a deceased person.
2. high praise or commendation."[1]

The word is derived from two Greek words, *eu* (well) and *logos* (word); in other words; "to speak well of".[2] In the New Testament, we see this word written as *eulogeo*. Strong's Concordance translates it into our English word, "bless, blessing."[3] Eulogeo and its derivative, *eulogea,* are similar to the Hebrew *Barak,* which meant "to bless and to praise" in the Old Testament.[4]

In scripture, a eulogy was not addressed to someone who was deceased. In several Middle Eastern traditions, a blessing - or eulogy - for the living was given by the elder or a person of high stature. Why was it so important to receive this blessing?

It was considered the pronouncement of the future, the

pronouncement of inheritance, and the setting up of the hierarchy of leadership within a clan or tribe. Below are four well-known instances of the spoken blessing.

In Genesis 27, we are given the account of Isaac blessing Esau and Jacob. According to Hebrew tradition, the father would give the primary blessing to the oldest son and would pass along the Covenant which began with Abraham (But if you are familiar with the account, Esau lost his birthright as the firstborn to his younger brother, Jacob).

Jacob, in turn, bestowed his blessing upon his sons in Genesis 48 and 49 (Of special note is the unique blessing Jacob bestowed upon Judah).

David blessed Solomon before his passing in 1 Kings 2, as was the Hebrew custom for kings.

In Matthew 19 we find the unique account of Jesus receiving the children to lay hands on them and pray. Many Bible scholars see this action as an account of His bestowing blessings upon them.

Throughout the scriptures, the concept of blessing was meant to build others up, to encourage them, and to motivate them.

I believe today's key verse is the true and proper place for the eulogy. In Ephesians 4:29, Paul wrote, *"Let no corrupt word proceed out of your mouth, but what is good for necessary edification, that it may impart grace to the hearers."*

Paul challenges us to edify others with our speech; in other words, speak only what is good to build up another. In today's social media-influenced society, we find the enemy has corrupted what could be a beautiful tool to build up others. More often than not, we see people using the written word to tear others down. We are losing the gift of giving a spoken (or written) blessing.

However, as federal and regional responses to the virus forced many of us to step back from our normal lives and interactions, we were compelled to consider new ways to communicate and influence. Now, more than ever, we should return to the gift of the spoken blessing!

Quoting from *Handoff*, Myers wrote:
> "When someone speaks a word of blessing to me, it's like a sincere hug to the soul...To receive a blessing is to be released from the insincere expectations of society. To give a blessing is to set others free."[5]

As you ponder today's devotion, I encourage you to practice being a healing balm, and a light in the darkness.

1. Build up those around you. Speak blessings into their lives!
     a. Be intentional to speak life ~ Ephesians 4:29
     b. Follow Christ's command to *"bless those who curse you, bless and do not curse."* ~ Matthew 5:44
2. *"Be diligent to speak the Truth in love"* ~ Ephesians 4:15. In order to do so, you may need to heed the words of James.
3. *"Be swift to hear, slow to speak, slow to wrath".* ~ James 1:19
4. Say only what is good for building up others ~ Ephesians 4:29

When you seek to intentionally do this, you will find a blessing in store for you.

1. Relationships will be stronger, because you will build

love into your speech, and meaning into your words.

2. Don't flatter but be intentional about finding the good to build upon.
3. If you must challenge another, allow Scripture to speak for itself, not your opinion.

Now is the appropriate time to speak a blessing into another. Let's not wait until it is too late!

Questions

1. Have you experienced a "eulogy" of a living person before?
2. If so, what was the setting?
3. Do you practice offering praise and uplifting speech to those around you?
4. Is there a person in your current sphere of influence who could use a "eulogy?"

Further Reading
Matthew 5:44; James 1:19

Notes

References

1. https://www.dictionary.com/browse/eulogy
2. *Handoff,* (Dr. Jeff Myers), page 63
3. Strong, James, "Eulogio." The New Strong's Expanded Exhaustive Concordance of the Bible, Thomas Nelson, 2001, Greek Dictionary of the New Testament, 2127, pp. 105-106
4. Strong, James, "Barak" The New Strong's Expanded Exhaustive Concordance of the Bible, Thomas Nelson, 2001, Hebrew and Aramaic Dictionary, 1288, *pp 46-47*
5. Myers, page 71.

Dr. Jeff Myers is considered one of America's most respected authorities on youth leadership development. He currently serves as the president of Summit Ministries. His book Handoff *is available through Amazon press.*

19.

COHESION

Therefore if there is any consolation in Christ, if any comfort of love, if any fellowship of the Spirit, if any affection and mercy, fulfill my joy by being like-minded, having the same love, being of one accord, of one mind.
Philippians 2:1-2

In his book, *The 17 Indisputable Laws of Teamwork,* John Maxwell states,

> "There is an old saying when it comes to teamwork: either we are pulling together or we're pulling apart. One Navy SEAL put it this way; 'Unit cohesion…means you have a pride (sic) in the ability of your group to function at a higher level than possible for the individual. The unit doesn't shine because you are a member, you shine because you're good enough to be a member.'" [1]

While my primary sport was track and field, my senior year of college I was given the opportunity to realize a childhood dream to play college football. During that season, I found Maxwell's axiom to be so true. I can recall the different layers of connection that were necessary for any play to function, whether on offense or defense. To run an offensive play, the timing and initiation of the play had to be synchronized to the cadence of the quarterback. Sometimes it was a verbal cadence. It could also be a specific count or other signal. The 10 teammates had to know the precise cadence in order not to jump offsides. The center, guards, and tackles had to know their specific assignments, and exactly how to execute those assignments in conjunction with their teammates. Receivers had specific routes layered upon each other, and the backfield either assisted in the blocking scheme or ran release routes of their own. When executed well, the team appears as one choreographed unit, performing with a purpose. A successful running back or quarterback understood that their success was due to the coordinated effort of the entire unit.

Paul, in his letter to the Philippian church, addresses bickering that was occurring among its members. He lays out the groundwork for his exhortation beginning in 1:27 when he writes,

> *"Only let your conduct be worthy of the gospel of Christ, so that whether I come and see you or am absent, I may hear of your affairs, that you stand fast in one spirit, with one mind striving together for the faith of the gospel."*

The Greek phrase for 'striving together' literally means "to engage together in an athletic event." The idea was that all should learn how to function as a team. The challenge for the Philippian church applies today as well. As the Body of Christ, we must learn to function with the cohesion of a great team. We each must be fully on board, bringing our specific gifts and talents to fulfill our God-given assignment. We also must depend on the gifts and talents of others as we work alongside them. Pride must be set aside for the sake of the body.

In this age of individualism, the challenge is for us to set aside our personal ambitions and be a part of the team. As Paul wrote,

> *"Let nothing be done through selfish ambition or conceit, but in lowliness of mind let each esteem others better than himself. Let each of you look out not only for his own interests, but also for the interests of others."* ~ Philippians 2:3-4

We have a God-sized assignment, to go into the world and make disciples. We cannot do it alone. Only as we work together and submit to Christ's authority, can we do so. As we do, we will fulfill Paul's challenge in Philippians 2:5-11.

"Let this mind be in you which was also in Christ Jesus, who, being in the form of God, did not consider it robbery to be equal with God, but made Himself of no reputation, taking the form of a bondservant, and coming in the likeness of men. And being found in appearance as a man, He humbled Himself and became obedient to the point of death, even the death of the cross. Therefore, God also has highly exalted Him and given Him the name which is above every name, that at the name of Jesus every knee should bow, of those in heaven, and of those on earth, and of those under the earth, and that every tongue should confess that Jesus Christ is Lord, to the glory of God the Father."

Questions

1. Do your goals align with the goals of the team?
2. Read Philippians 2:3 again. What does this tell us about how we should view ourselves?
3. What are three tangible ways you can help your team practice and compete with more cohesion and synergy?

Further Reading

2 Corinthians 12; Ephesians 4:1-17

Notes

References

1. Maxwell, John C. *The 17 Indisputable Laws of Teamwork*. 1 ed., Nashville, Thomas Nelson Publishing, 2003

20.

CLOUT

Now all things are of God, who has reconciled us to Himself through Jesus Christ, and has given us the ministry of reconciliation, [19] that is, that God was in Christ reconciling the world to Himself, not imputing their trespasses to them, and has committed to us the word of reconciliation.
2 Corinthians 5: 18-19

As 2019 drew to a close, the Associated Press proclaimed World and Olympic Gymnastics Champion Simone Biles the Female Athlete of the Year.[1] Biles had dominated the sport the previous 3 years, proving herself to be the best overall, and in several apparatuses. However, it was not her athletic prominence that earned her a second Athlete of the Year award – this time in a non-Olympic year. It was how she chose to use her status for good.

Biles became a prominent agent for change when she chose to become an advocate for sexual abuse survivors – herself included – in the wake of the Larry Nassar sexual abuse scandal and the complete upheaval and overhaul of USA gymnastics. In an ESPN article about the award, Biles commented,

> "I realize now with the platform I have it will be powerful if I speak up and speak for what I believe in. It's an honor to speak for those that are less fortunate. So if I can be a voice for them in a positive manner, then of course I'm going to do whatever I can."[1]

The combination of courage, perseverance, wisdom, and grace she displayed throughout the scandal is an indication of her character. Her determined decision to embrace her worldwide clout reminds me of a young Jewish maiden named Hadassah. This young lady rose to prominence in the court of the Persian king Ahasuerus, when she was selected to become the queen. Being queen carried some clout, but not the power to make decisions. In fact, she could never simply walk into the king's presence unless summoned – anyone who chose to do so was put to death.

As she served in this role, it became known to a certain family member that there was a plot to destroy the Jews in the kingdom, unbeknownst to the king. When news of the decree reached her, Hadassah reached out to this relative – a cousin named Mordecai. He convinced the young queen to intercede on behalf of the Jewish people, though it might cost her life. He challenged this queen, whose Persian name is Esther, with these words:

"Do not think in your heart that you will escape in the king's palace any more than all the other Jews. [14] For if you remain completely silent at this time, relief and deliverance will arise for the Jews from another place, but you and your father's house will perish. Yet who knows whether you have come to the kingdom for such a time as this?"
~Esther 4:13-14

We all love the phrase, "for such a time as this." However, I think sometimes we forget just how high the cost could be for Esther. Her life would be forfeited if she remained silent. It could also be forfeited if she chose to speak up. I find her response to be even more powerful:

"Go, gather all the Jews who are present in Shushan, and fast for me; neither eat nor drink for three days, night or day. My maids and I will fast likewise. And so I will go to the king, which is against the law; and

if I perish, I perish!" ~Esther 4:16

Mordecai helped Esther understand the platform she had to be an agent for change. She grasped how much it could cost her. In her choice, she displayed the same courage, strength, wisdom, and grace we saw in Simone Biles. God worked through her to save the nation of Israel.

Athletes and coaches have tremendous opportunity and power through their platform of sport. In 2020, we continue to see athletes trying to use their platforms for causes important to them. Biles's role in the aftermath of the scandal is highly commendable. However, as Christian athletes and coaches, our calling is even more sacred. We are to be set apart for God's purposes, and we will be accountable before Christ for our work. We may not be given the same platform as a professional athlete. However, whether it is in a college gym, a recreation center pool, or a little league field, we have the opportunity to impact many people in our communities.

1 Peter 3:15 says,

> *But sanctify the Lord God in your hearts, and* **always be ready to give a defense** *to everyone who asks you a reason for the hope that is in you, with meekness and fear; ¹⁶ having a good conscience, that when they defame you as evildoers, those who revile your good conduct in Christ may be ashamed.* (emphasis mine)

Regardless of the potential outcome, no matter the cost, Christ calls us to use the platform He has provided us for His glory. Never forget Paul's words to the Corinthians,

> *"Now then, we are ambassadors for Christ, as though God were pleading through us: we implore you on Christ's behalf, be reconciled to God."* ~2 Corinthians 5:20

Questions

1. Name some different causes for which you have seen professional athletes and coaches advocate?
2. Have you ever used your standing as an athlete or coach to do good?
3. In what ways can you use your current platform to draw others into a relationship with Christ?

Further Reading

Read the entire book of Esther for greater perspective on her endearing role.
2 Corinthians 5:12-21

Notes

References

1. "Simone Soars: Biles names 2019 Female Athlete of the Year" Will Graves, Dec. 26, 2019.
https://apnews.com/article/a8b2e5417016d5c39a52315890037c29

21.

MIRY CLAY

He also brought me up out of a horrible pit,
Out of the miry clay,
And set my feet upon a rock,
And established my steps.
Psalm 40:2

During the summer months of my high school and college years, I worked for my family's concrete company to pay for college. My first couple of years, I was not allowed in the "mud," the term older workers used when talking about wet concrete. I can remember my first experience when I was finally allowed to join the workers in the wet concrete as we laid an airport landing pad. Prior to the experience, my foreman instructed me to buy dairy boots for getting into the concrete, and to have a few sets of pants set aside for "mud days."

That specific day, I recall the final preparations as we awaited the concrete truck. We checked our forms, confirmed depths, and laid out our equipment in advance; concrete trucks were hired by the hour. We knew we had a specific time frame to complete the process before the concrete hardened too much. We needed to be very efficient with our time.

When the truck pulled up, we quickly grabbed our gear and put on our boots. As we began to shovel and push the concrete around the area, I found myself in the middle of the 8-inch-deep concrete with an older worker. As we progressed, he deftly stepped out of the mud and moved further down the line. As I sought to follow him, I realized my foot was stuck in concrete above my ankles. I tried to heave my leg out. As I did, I pulled my foot out of my boot, leaving the boot in the wet concrete. Standing on one foot, I tried to pull the boot out. Unfortunately, I lost my balance, placing my hand and my socked foot into the mud as I tried to keep from falling face first. The older workers chuckled as a fellow worker reached in, picked me up and placed me out of the concrete before retrieving my boot. As I put my boot back on in embarrassment, my foreman told me not to be embarrassed, as they had all experienced the same at some time. I learned a lot that day about working in the mud!

When I see today's scripture, it takes me back to that particular experience. "Miry Clay" might be better described as boggy, marshy, waterlogged mud. If you have ever experienced walking through a marshy area, you understand that it can be very dangerous. The mud not only holds you in place, it will suck a person down if it is too deep. Any effort to remove yourself results in being pulled further in. Many animal remains have been found in marshlands after suffering the slow, lonely, suffocating, and desperate fight to escape.

Just as I know how difficult it is to remove myself from the wet concrete, many of us struggle with burdens in our own personal walks. We hear so many stories from addicts about the difficulty they faced when seeking to overcome their vice. It is true for all of us.

In his devotional blog, "Getting Out of the Miry Clay," Bishop George Bloomer stated,

> "Perhaps you're facing distressing circumstances in your life today. Whether because of your own foolish choices or situations beyond your control,

you've found yourself in 'a horrible pit' filled with 'miry clay.'"*(1)*

He continued, "The longer you've been stuck in a situation, the harder it usually is to break free – mostly because we've become entrenched in a mindset of failure and futility."[1]

David faced such a time in his life. In Psalm 40: 1-4, he cried out to the Lord for deliverance, and found our Redeemer God waiting to lift him and set him on solid ground. There are a few points to ponder:

1. David had to remain patient through the trial.
2. His patience was based upon his confidence in the Almighty God.
3. God does hear the cries of His children.
4. God – not David – lifted him out of the clay; too often, we believe we can save ourselves if we just "work harder" or have a strong enough "will."
5. God established David's steps.
6. God gave him a NEW song!

If you are a believer struggling in the pit of despair, floundering in the miry clay of life, call to Jesus. Cry out to the Lord of life. He hears His own.

If you don't know God through His son, Jesus Christ, I encourage you to learn of Him through His Word for us, and submit to His absolute authority in your life. For *"whoever calls on the name of the Lord shall be saved."* ~Romans 10:13

Questions

1. Have you ever experienced walking through deep mud? If so, how did it hinder your walking?
2. Do you recall a time when circumstances drew you to a dark place in your life? How did you make it through those times?
3. How can David's words equip and strengthen you to stay focused on your journey?

Further Reading

Psalm 27; Isaiah 41:10; Matthew 28:20

Notes

References

1. Bloomer, George. "Getting Out of Miry Clay." *Inspiration.org*, 2001-2026, https://inspiration.org/christian-articles/getting-out-of-the-miry-clay/. Accessed 5 August 2020.

22.

RAISING THE BAR: PART 1 - AIM HIGHER

But also for this very reason, giving all diligence, add to your faith virtue, to virtue knowledge, to knowledge self-control, to self-control perseverance, to perseverance godliness, to godliness brotherly kindness, and to brotherly kindness love. For if these things are yours and abound, you will be neither barren nor unfruitful in the knowledge of our Lord Jesus Christ.
2 Peter 1:5-8

An FCA Devotion originally attributed to former Olympian and former American high jump record-holder Hollis Conway states:

> "It is quite simply a thing of beauty to see the competitors in this event propel their bodies over a bar suspended almost eight feet in the air. It seems so effortless."[1]

In the sports realm, there are only two events which physically require the raising of a bar to increase the level of competition: the pole vault and high jump. As a former high school jumper, I was mesmerized by those jumpers and vaulters capable of competing for the world record. I also can vividly recall my own mix of emotions each time I efficiently executed a jump and cleared the bar. There was a budding elation and a sense of accomplishment each time the bar was raised. There was also a growing anxiety as the bar neared, equaled, then surpassed my personal best. Those collective emotions could result in one of two outcomes (until the bar was ultimately set beyond my physical capabilities). I either:

a) allowed the anxiety to dominate my thoughts, lost my focus, and failed to execute well at the next height or

b) used the elation and confidence gained from success to override the anxiety, which resulted in a renewed focus and diligence to execute even better.

Regardless of which internal approach prevailed, raising the bar raised the expectations and standards required for execution.

The idiom "raise the bar," and all of its spin-offs, was first coined in the early 1900's, a direct result of renewed competition in the high jump and pole vault. According to grammarist.com, it means "to set a high standard, to raise expectations, to set higher goals."[2]

Scripture encourages and challenges us to raise the bar in our faith journey. In today's passage, Peter encourages believers with these words:

"add to your faith virtue, to virtue knowledge, to knowledge self-control, to self-control perseverance, to perseverance godliness, to godliness brotherly kindness, and to brotherly kindness love."
~2 Peter 1:5-7

Believers were never expected to attain all of these qualities at once. Sadly, many of us may have adapted such a misunderstanding once we accepted Christ. When I embraced a relationship with Christ at age 17, I quickly came back to earth when I realized I was still the same rebellious teen I had been, with the same bent towards sin. I had not learned that I had to actively and intentionally "put off the old man and put on the new man" (from Ephesians 4:22-24 and Colossians 3:8-10). I did not have many of the character traits seen in this passage, nor the fruits of the spirit found in Galatians 5:22-23. My journey was just beginning. As I grew in my faith, I began to see the emergence of new qualities and fruits. Oftentimes, they were developed in the crucible of trial. I also realized that as I grew, I would endure a new set of growing pains in order to add a new virtue. I came to a new understanding of Paul's encouraging words in Philippians 1:6, "*that He who has begun a good work in you will complete it until the day of Jesus Christ.*"

As we continue our journey with Christ, He challenges us to raise the bar in our walk with Him. We must continually put off the old and put on the new. Each time we take a step forward, Christ will raise the bar for us to continue growing. We don't accomplish this growth alone; He has empowered us with the presence of His Holy Spirit. When the bar is raised, we will be challenged again to submit to Christ's Lordship and the power of the Holy Spirit.

Let's take the challenge and raise the bar in our lives!

Questions

1. Recall your experience training for competition. How did the process of training stimulate growth in you as an athlete?
2. Recall a time when personal trials led your faith to grow and mature.
3. In hindsight, what are some perspectives you now maintain regarding trials?

Further Reading
1 Corinthians 9:24-27; Ephesians 4:17-24
Philippians 3:13-14

Notes

References
1. FCA Resources. "Raising the Bar Devotion." *FCA Resources*, Fellowship of Christian Athletes, 2018, https://fcaresources.com/devotional/raising-bar. Accessed 3 21 2018.
2. Grammarist. "Raise the bar idiom." *grammarist.com*, 2009-2014, https://grammarist.com/idiom/raise-the-bar/. Accessed 1 4 2018.

23.

RAISING THE BAR: PART 2 - PUT ON THE NEW

Do not lie to one another, since you have put off the old man with his deeds, and have put on the new man who is renewed in knowledge according to the image of Him who created him.
Colossians 3:9-10

One of the most fulfilling times in college coaching is seeing players have the opportunity to fulfill a dream. On draft day, that special moment when a player holds up the jersey of his new professional team symbolizes the transition in that player's life. They shed their old jersey for their new team and new life.

This sports image is a great object lesson of today's passage, where Paul reminds the Colossian believers that they have already cast off the old man and put on the new.

He shares similar encouragement in Ephesians 4:20-24;
> *"But you have not so learned Christ, if indeed you have heard Him and have been taught by Him, as the truth is in Jesus: that you put off, concerning your former conduct, the old man which grows corrupt according to the deceitful lusts, and be renewed in the spirit of your mind, and that you put on the new man which was created according to God, in true righteousness and holiness."*

He had just challenged the Ephesians that they *"should no longer walk as the rest of the Gentiles walk, in the futility of their mind."* ~ Ephesians 4:17

Verse 17 can be a hard concept to grasp if we come to faith later in life. Intellectually, we may understand 2 Corinthians 5:17 which states, *"Therefore, if anyone is in Christ, he is a new creation; old things have passed away; behold, all things have become new."*

But how do we *live in the "new?"* The first step in our faith is the same step a jumper takes as the bar is raised. We must be willing to take the risk in trusting God, just as jumper's faith rests in his training and his history in the event. The more experienced the jumper, the more confidence he has in his training. However, a new jumper has nothing to fall back upon but himself, and thus must rely on the assurance of his coach and of those who have gone before him. It is the same in our spiritual life. When we first place our faith in Christ, the Spirit comes alive within us. We may not have life experience in Him, but we do have the Word of God and the testimony of believers in scripture and life. Just as a coach has trained us to shed bad habits and adapt new, we must take the action of casting off daily old habits and beliefs, and adopting new ones.

How do we adopt new beliefs? Paul told the Ephesians to be *"renewed in the spirit of our minds."* That renewal takes place as we allow scripture to fill our lives through study, meditation and submission to its authority. The Holy Spirit will continue to grow in us as we give Him the lead. As we do, we find we are becoming more like Christ. When we fall into old habits, we have Paul's challenge and reminder that we have already cast aside the old jersey. We are on a new team. Raise the bar and put on the new!

Questions

1. In your personal athletic training, what were some old habits you had to discard in order to improve?
2. What steps did you take to remove those habits from your training? How difficult was it to make changes?
3. As you continue to grow in your faith, what are current issues, behaviors, or habits that God is challenging you to change? What steps will you take to make the needed change?

Further Reading
Romans 12:1-2; Colossians 3

Notes

24.

MAXIMIZING OPPORTUNITY: REDEEMING THE TIME

Walk in wisdom toward those who are outside, redeeming the time.
Colossians 4:5

In 2011, NFL WR Antonio Brown became the first receiver in NFL history to eclipse 1000 yards in both returns and receiving in the same year. At one point in his career, he was the highest-paid receiver in the league, an acknowledgement of his value to his team and the game.

When asked about his receptions in one interview, he commented, "I don't have a number, I just want to catch them all. That's always my goal is to maximize every opportunity and every throw that's coming my way."[1]

In Paul's epistles to the churches at Colossae and Ephesus, Paul exhorted both churches with similar challenges. He encouraged the Colossians, "*Walk in wisdom toward those who are outside, redeeming   the   time. Let your   speech   always be with grace, seasoned with salt, that you may know how you ought to answer each one.*" ~ Colossians 4:5-6.

Similarly, he urged the Ephesian church, "*See then that you walk circumspectly, not as fools but as wise, redeeming the time, because the days are evil.*" ~ Ephesians 5:15-16

In both epistles, Paul used the Greek word, *exagorazo,* which means "to ransom, to rescue from loss." Paul paired *exagorazo* with the Greek word "*Kairos,*" for time. In this context, *Strong's Concordance's* expanded translation reads, **"making the most of every opportunity (Kairos), turning each to the best advantage since none can be recalled if missed."**[2] (emphasis mine)

Paul was instructing both churches how to live out their faith. Likewise, he challenges all believers to walk in the wisdom that comes from Christ. We embrace Godly wisdom as we apply His Word to our daily lives. It influences what we say, what we do, and what we believe.

As coaches and athletes, we want to make the most of our opportunities in our particular venue. In 2020, we were all reminded that those opportunities are not guaranteed. Don't take your opportunities for granted.

Christian, now is the time to maximize your opportunity. You are given today. Make the most of it!

Questions

1. Can you recall an athletic moment when you were able to capitalize on an opportunity?
2. What was required to make the most of that moment?
3. How do we maximize our daily opportunities to grow in our faith?
4. How do we maximize our daily opportunities to serve others?

Further Reading
Ecclesiastes 11; Romans 12:1-8

Notes

References
1. "Antonio Brown Quotes." BrainyQuote.com. BrainyMedia Inc, 2020. 1 April 2020.
   https://www.brainyquote.com/quotes/antonio_brown_868339
2. James Strong, LL.D, and S.T.D. and John R. Kohlberger III. "Redeem." *The New Strong's Expanded Exhaustive Concordance of the Bible, Red Letter Edition,* Thomas Nelson, 2001, p. 710.

25.

BE HOLY (SET APART)

But as He who called you is holy, you also be holy in
all your conduct, because it is written, "Be holy, for I am holy."
1 Peter 1:15-16

College athletes live a life set apart. Regardless of whether one views it from a negative light ("Athletes seem to get special treatment") or a positive light ("athletes live a disciplined life"), it is a reality. Athletes endure discipline to develop physical strength and hone skills necessary to compete at a high level. Athletes set aside chunks of their days, weeks, and months to focus on training and competitions. Athletes persevere through the pain of off-season and preseason conditioning and training. These programs may break the uncommitted athlete, but the disciplined athlete emerges refined, equipped and polished.

Often when people read 1 Peter 1:15, they balk at the notion of "being holy." Their response is a reflection of an inadequate understanding of the word "holy." It is often due to the world's skewed view of Christianity and the world's lack of understanding of Christ's commands through scripture.

However, holiness is about being set apart, not being better. The Greek word, *hagios*, fundamentally means *being set apart, or separated.*[1] God Himself is holy. He is set apart from sin. His thoughts are not our thoughts, His ways are not our ways (Isaiah 55:8) Christ is distinctly set apart from all earthly beings, as Philippians 2:9 and Colossians 1:15-16 proclaim. He calls us to become like Himself, as we rely on the Holy

Spirit to transform us.

Paul gives us an illustration of being set apart in 2 Timothy 2:20-21. *The Message* version expresses it in modern terms:

"In a well-furnished kitchen there are not only crystal goblets and silver platters, but waste cans and compost buckets—some containers used to serve fine meals, others to take out the garbage. Become the kind of container God can use to present any and every kind of gift to his guests for their blessing."[2]

Many of us probably own fine china and/or crystal, set in a place of honor and used for special occasions. Once used, we take great care to clean them delicately, and set them aside again for future use.

To Christ, we are His fine china.

In 1 Peter 2:9-10, he proclaims,

"But you are a chosen generation, a royal priesthood, a holy nation, His own special people, that you may proclaim the praises of Him who called you out of darkness into His marvelous light; who once were not a people but are now the people of God, who had not obtained mercy but now have obtained mercy."

We do not need to fear the phrase "be Holy." Through daily submission to the Word of God, through the power of the Holy Spirit and prayer, and through daily decisions to live life according to God's guidance, we are being transformed and set apart for a beautiful work.

Be holy. Be set apart. Break away from the pack!

Questions

1. Recall your own experience with sports. What steps were you required to take to set yourself apart for your sport?
2. What steps do you take in your daily life to set yourself apart for Christ?

Further Reading

Romans 12:1-2; 1 Corinthians 3:12-17
Jeremiah 18:1-11

Notes

References

1. Strong, James. *The New Strong's Expanded Exhaustive Concordance of the Bible*. Red Letter ed., Nashville, TN, Thomas Nelson, 2001.
2. Scripture quotations marked MSG are taken from THE MESSAGE, copyright © 1993, 2002, 2018 by Eugene H. Peterson. Used by permission of NavPress, represented by Tyndale House Publishers. All rights reserved.

26.

PRESSING ON: PART 1 - PASSION, POISE, PURPOSE

"I press toward the goal for the prize of the upward call of God in Christ Jesus."
Philippians 3:14

The night of February 23, 2008, a packed crowd and ESPN audience witnessed a marquee men's basketball game, a perfect contest featuring the top two teams in the nation. Bruce Pearl led the #2 Tennessee Vols to a 66-62 victory over the #1 Memphis Tigers coached by John Calipari. During pre-game, Vols' Coach Bruce Pearl motivated his players with these words:

"Passion, poise, and purpose! Passion, poise, and purpose allow us to win on the road. We are going to play with passion. But we are going to have poise when they make their run; poise when they block shots; poise when they talk to us; poise when it gets elevated a bit. 'Cause everything we do, we do with a purpose. When we guard, when we rebound, when we fast break, and when we execute!"[1]

Through the seesaw match, his team displayed all three, playing passionately, remaining poised when Memphis made their first seven three-pointers, and playing with one purpose: to win.

As Christians, we often we stumble in the midst of adversity or lose heart due to persecution. We lose sight of the scriptural truth in Ephesians 2:10 that we are *"His workmanship, created in Christ Jesus for good works, which God prepared beforehand that we should walk in them."*

The Bible offers us the testimonies of believers who passionately fulfilled God's purpose, even in the midst of adversity. Paul eloquently asserts his passion, poise and purpose in Philippians 3.

PASSION

Paul's passion was palpable when he proclaimed, *"Yet indeed I also count all things loss for the excellence of the knowledge of Christ Jesus my Lord, for whom I have suffered the loss of all things, and count them as rubbish, that I may gain Christ"* ~ Philippians 3:8

He gave us a great example of living with passion. His passion for Christ and passion for others to know Him permeates every word of his epistles. He constantly challenges us to *"run in such a way as to receive the prize."* ~1 Corinthians 9:24 (NIV)[2]

POISE

His poise was unmistakable to those around him, including the guards at the Roman prison where he was chained. In Philippians 1:13 Paul proclaims, *"my imprisonment in the cause of Christ has become well known throughout the praetorian guard and to everyone else."*

Although chained for his proclamation of the gospel, Paul did not lose heart or shy away from the task set before him. He proclaimed to the church at Corinth,

> *"We are hard-pressed on every side, yet not crushed; we are perplexed, but not in despair; persecuted, but not forsaken; struck down, but not destroyed— always carrying about in*

the body the dying of the Lord Jesus, that the life of Jesus also may be manifested in our body."
~ 2 Corinthians 4:8-10

PURPOSE

Paul was beaten, stoned, dragged out of town, and imprisoned for his proclamation of the gospel. Yet he endured the adversity, persecution and imprisonment because he was determined to proclaim the gospel and thus complete the race Christ set before him. In another epistle to the Colossians, he wrote, *"pray also for us, that God may open to us a door for the word, to declare the mystery of Christ, on account of which I am in prison"* ~ Colossians 4:3 (ESV)

As athletes and coaches, many of us can understand playing with the passion, poise, and purpose that Coach Pearl talked about. Are we willing to devote our lives fully to running "the race" with that same passion for Christ, poise under fire, and single-mindedness of purpose? Let's order our steps so that we can complete the race Christ has set for us. Then, when our task is complete, we can echo Paul's words and say *"I have fought the good fight, I have finished the race, I have kept the faith."* ~2 Timothy 4:7

Questions

1. Are there areas of your Christian walk for which you lack passion?
2. What are some areas of your life where you have lost heart or desire?
3. Pick one of Paul's epistles and read with the three keys of today's devotion in mind. Pray for God to show you how you can strengthen your faith to live with passion, poise, and purpose.

Further Reading

Read the testimony of others who lived with poise, passion, and purpose:
Esther chapters 1-9; Daniel 3

Notes

References

1. ESPN broadcast. "Tennessee vs. Memphis." *Youtube*, 23 February 2008, https://www.youtube.com/watch?v=BWhwxlqD9RA. Accessed 23 February 2008.
2. "Scripture quotations marked (NIV) are taken from the Holy Bible, New International Version®, NIV®. Copyright © 1973, 1978, 1984, 2011 by Biblica, Inc.™ Used by permission of Zondervan. All rights reserved worldwide. www.zondervan.comThe "NIV" and "New International Version" are trademarks registered in the United States Patent and Trademark Office by Biblica, Inc.™"
https://www.zondervan.com/about-us/permissions/#:~:text=Scripture%20quotations%20marked%20(NIV,Office%20by%20Biblica%2C%20Inc.%E2%84%A2

27.

PRESSING ON: PART 2 -
THE JOHN STEPHEN AHKWARI STORY

Brethren, I do not count myself to have apprehended; but one thing I do, forgetting those things which are behind and reaching forward to those things which are ahead, I press toward the goal for the prize of the upward call of God in Christ Jesus.
Philippians 3:13-14

Growing up, I fell in love with the Olympics through the work of Bud Greenspan. Greenspan produced a series titled "The Olympiad," a multi-segment documentary with various stories about Olympic athletes.

One particular segment that resonated with me was the story of John Stephen Ahkwari. Ahkwari, a Tanzanian marathoner, competed in the 1968 Olympics.

His is not the story of victory, but of perseverance. During the race, he struggled through severe cramps as well as a dislocated knee, deep leg gash, and shoulder injury resulting from a collision and fall. Most observers expected him to quit, but he received quick medical attention and limped on. Slowed by the injury, there was no chance of obtaining a medal or eclipsing his own person best. However, he refused to quit. Ahkwari crossed the finish line long after other competitors had finished, in the darkness of night. Gold medalist Mamo Wolde had already received his gold medal when Awkwari, with a bloodied bandage falling from his leg, limped his way around the track for his final lap. Commentators stated that although most of the crowd had left, those who remained gave him a standing ovation for that final lap. When asked after the race why he did not quit, he responded, "My country did not send me 5,000 miles to start the race, they sent me 5,000 miles to finish the race." [1] With the uncertainty of our times, it would be easy to pull away from everything. However, we were not chosen to simply start a task. We are chosen to complete a specific, God-ordained body of work.

We have a unique opportunity to pass along the baton of faith to others at a unique time in history. 2020 did not unfold as any of us envisioned. However, trust that God's plan for you, with your unique personality, gifts, and calling, will be fulfilled in His time.

Hebrews 12: 1-2 reads,

> *"Therefore we also, since we are surrounded by so great a cloud of witnesses, let us lay aside every weight, and the sin which so easily ensnares us, and let us run with endurance the race that is set before us, looking unto Jesus, the author and finisher of our faith, who for the joy that was set before Him endured the cross, despising the shame, and has sat down at the right hand of the throne of God."*

Let's keep in mind those that have gone before us, those who influence our lives, and those who built our programs. Let's remember we are laying a foundation for the next generation of faith. We are in crunch time. As a former hurdler, I was always taught to look beyond the hurdle in front of me. We must do the same. We must cast our eyes to the finish line. Christ has our backs. Christ goes before us. Christ will be waiting for us at the end of our journey.

Stay the course and press on.

Questions

1. What struggles have you faced in your own life? How were you directly affected by unusual calamity in your life (such as 2020)?
2. How do you utilize God's Word to cope with calamity in your life?
3. What lessons have you learned from those difficulties?

Further Reading

Philippians 3; Hebrews 12:1-3
1 Peter 3:8-22

Notes

References

1. Tomizawa, John. "John Akhwari and His last place finish." *The Olympians*, 20 May 2016, https://theolympians.co/2016/05/20/john-akhwari-champions-do-finish-last/#:~:text=All%20honor%20to%20John%20Stephen,5%2C000%20miles%20to%20finish%20it.%E2%80%9D]. Accessed 26 March 2020.

28.

UNITY

I, therefore, the prisoner of the Lord, beseech you to walk worthy of the calling with which you were called, with all lowliness and gentleness, with longsuffering, bearing with one another in love, endeavoring to keep the unity of the Spirit in the bond of peace.
Ephesians 4:1-3

My freshman year of college, I attended a school which had a crew (rowing) program. I became fascinated with the sport, as several close friends were a part of the team. I was amazed at the amount of intentional team building that occurred in preseason. As I grew in my understanding of the team component and the specific roles and responsibilities of each team member, I realized how essential unity was for each boat crew to be successful.

Unity is at the core of every successful program in any team sport, which has been noted by business leaders for years. There are several quotes I gathered over the years that highlight the importance of unity:

> "Unity is strength…when there is teamwork and collaboration, wonderful things can be achieved." ~ Mattie J.T. Stepanek[1]

> "The strength of the team is each member. The strength of each member is the team." ~ Phil Jackson[2]

> "A boat doesn't go forward if each one is rowing

their own way." ~ Swahili Proverb[3]

One concept that attracted me to the athletics department at Grove City College was our theme "Wolverines Together," an intentional challenge to build unity in our shared endeavor to glorify God through excellence on and off the playing field. The intention was to develop a common bond that ran deeper than athletic allegiance. Just as "Wolverines Together" served as a call to unite my athletics department, Paul encourages us with the words from today's passage.

As the Church expanded during the first century, God impressed upon the apostles the critical need to maintain unity in their calling. It is obvious this was a challenge throughout the Church, as similar appeals are seen in several other epistles. As we look at the modern Church, we can see that divisions still exist. We see it in denominational battles, music culture wars, racial, ethnic, and political issues. Sadly, the world often does not see us as one Church body, but as a divided kingdom. We ought not wonder why our voice is not considered relevant today.

In today's society, we have common, everyday object lessons that can remind us of the importance of biblical unity. We see it every day we observe team sports. Just as I, a multi-sport athlete, learned tremendous lessons as I investigated the world of crew, we too can be reminded of God's call for unity. Redemption will not come to this world if it does not start with us. We first must unite under the banner of Christ and in full agreement over God's infallible truths provided by scripture, heeding the words of 2 Chronicles 7:14

> *"if my people who are called by my name humble themselves, and pray and seek my face and turn from their wicked ways, then I will hear from heaven and will forgive their sin and heal their land."*

We can unite as one when we put into practice what Paul proclaimed in today's passage:

- Intolerance and pride divide; but **patience and humility** unite.
- An insensitive, selfish heart divides; but a **kind, gentle** spirit unites.
- Accusations and condemnation divide; but **forgiveness** unites.
- Hate divides; Love unites.

In this time of discord and disunity, let us work to unite as the people of God so that we may fulfill God's great commission and teach the world of His great love.

Questions

1. What are some issues that destroy team unity?
2. How have you seen teams overcome such issues and develop a sense of unity?
3. What steps can you take to build unity in the body of Christ today?

Further Reading
1 Corinthians 3; 1 Corinthians 12
Ephesians 4; Philippians 2:1-18

Notes

References
1. "Mattie Stepanek - Unity is Strength." BrainyQuotes.com, BrainyMedia, INC, 2017, https://www.brainyquote.com/quotes/mattie_stepanek_319300. Accessed 7 7 2020.
2. Goodreads, Inc. "Quote by Phil Jackson." *Goodreads.com*, 2017, https://www.goodreads.com/quotes/527132-the-strength-of-the-team-is-each-individual-member-the. Accessed 7 7 2020.
3. "African Proverbs." *Slife.org*, 2020, https://slife.org/african-proverbs/. Accessed 7 7 2020.

29.

SPIRITUAL MARKERS

I am reminded of your sincere faith, a faith that dwelt first in your grandmother Lois and your mother Eunice and now, I am sure, dwells in you as well.
2 Timothy 1:5 (ESV)

My wife and I love to hike, a shared experience since our courtship years. We have experienced hiking trails throughout the country. We often joke about one particular early misadventure in the mountains of Southern California. We were attending a college function at our denominational campground and were hiking back from the nearby public lake. Unfortunately, there were trails from several other campgrounds that intersected our trail as well. The lack of clear trail displays made it difficult to ensure we stayed on the correct trail - thus, we took a wrong turn and returned later than expected.

I've always appreciated the colored trail marker system, which clearly indicates if you are on the correct trail or not. I learned through that early misadventure to recognize my particular trail, and to keep my eyes open for new trail markers. If I had doubts, I could also check over my shoulder to find trail markers we had previously passed to ensure I stayed on the correct trail.

In an earlier devotion, I stated the need to keep our eyes focused ahead. This is true. However, through my adult years I have come to the realization that God lays down markers in our lives to guide us and keep us on the right path when we have moments of doubt. In the Old Testament, He used feasts and festivals as reminders of His great work for the Israelites. Some of these markers also foreshadowed the work He was yet to do through the redemptive work of Christ (such as the Passover Supper).

I like to believe that God uses people as well as spiritual markers in our lives, as "living stones" being built up into a spiritual house (1 Peter 2:5). When Paul testifies of the faith of Lois and Eunice, he is pointing out spiritual markers for Timothy. He directs Timothy to this foundation of faith as he persuades Timothy to stir up the gifts which God deposited in Him. Paul follows this theme of reassurance and encouragement throughout this challenging second epistle to his protégé.

As I reflect on my own personal life, I can see the spiritual markers left behind by others. My praying grandmother, the grace of my mother, the support of my great-uncle, the example of a dear elderly couple as I prepared to marry, along with many others served as guides which pointed to Christ. Their impact on my life always points me forward, with a renewed focus on the prize of the upward call of Christ.

When you have moments of doubt, take a peek back at the spiritual markers in your life. Allow the testimonies of those individuals to point you forward. They are a small but vital portion of God's providential work for you. As the psalmist said in Psalm 77:11-12 (ESV),

> *"I will remember the deeds of the Lord;*
> *yes, I will remember your wonders of old.*
> *I will ponder all your work,*
> *and meditate on your mighty deeds."*

Stop, reflect, and refocus on your center in Christ. Then, face forward, reset your gaze, and continue on the path.

Questions

1. Who are the "living stones" God has placed in your life as spiritual markers?
2. How did they impact and focus your eyes on Christ?
3. To whom might you serve as a spiritual marker?

Further Reading
Hebrews 11; Psalm 77

Notes

30.

LEAVE A MARK

Then he spoke to the children of Israel, saying: "When your children ask their fathers in time to come, saying, 'What are these stones?' then you shall let your children know, saying, 'Israel crossed over this Jordan on dry land';
that all the peoples of the earth may know the hand of the Lord, that it is mighty, that you may fear the Lord your God forever."
Joshua 4:21-22, 24

As a child, I grew up in Southern California during the heyday of USC football and the end of the UCLA basketball dynasty. I can't recall visiting either campus when I was young, but I had the privilege as an adult to visit their famed venues. When I walked the halls of such storied programs, it was difficult not to recognize the markers of their journey from inception to excellence displayed through the pictures, banners, and trophies housed within.

As individuals, we probably have reminders of our own journeys. In my personal life, I have found music serves as a powerful marker, and I can trace most periods of my life through popular music. Athletically, pictures also serve as markers of great individuals, significant moments, and great achievements.

In the Old Testament, God used markers as well. The feasts and festivals all had significant meaning and pointed the Israelites to Him. At times He used physical markers as well, such as the memorial found in Joshua 4.

At the end of Deuteronomy, Moses was not allowed to cross over with the people and passed his leadership to Joshua. As Joshua was given authority over the emergent nation, God encouraged him with the words, "*Be strong and courageous*" ~ Joshua 1:9. Joshua's first action was to lead this group of sojourners across the Jordan river into the promised land.

Many are probably familiar with God's miraculous parting of the Red Sea as the Israelites fled Egypt (Ex 14:13-31). However, many people don't realize that God did the same for Joshua and Israel **as they crossed the Jordan**. Joshua chapter 3 documents this crossing.

As they crossed the Jordan, Israel left behind 400 years of slavery. They also left behind the lost generation who disobeyed God and were cursed to 40 years in the wilderness. In that moment at the Jordan river, this emergent nation was crossing a threshold into a new life. However, they had the tabernacle, the 10 commandments, and the first 5 books of scripture as a testament to God's work and a roadmap for the future. As they crossed, God had Joshua instruct the Israelites to leave one final mark.

"Then Joshua called the twelve men whom he had appointed from the children of Israel, one man from every tribe; and Joshua said to them: 'Cross over before the ark of the Lord your God into the midst of the Jordan, and each one of you take up a stone on his shoulder, according to the number of the tribes of the children of Israel, that this may be a sign among you when your children ask in time to come, saying, "What do these stones mean to you?"'
And the people of Israel did so, just as Joshua commanded."
~ Joshua 4:4-6, 8

After they completed the crossing, Joshua set up the 12 stones at Gilgal and proclaimed to the Israelites the scripture that opens this devotion, closing with the statement, "*that all the peoples of the earth may know the hand of the Lord, that it is mighty, that you may fear the Lord your God forever." ~* Joshua 4:24

As competitors and coaches, it is not wrong for us to hang banners, mount plaques, or display trophies, as long as we maintain a proper perspective. These markers will eventually rot and decay. However, they do mark the journey of our team and department.

As Christian coaches and athletes we should ask ourselves, what spiritual markers are we leaving behind as a testimony of God's work in our lives?

If we embrace our sport as a platform to serve God and others, we will find tremendous opportunity to see lives impacted for Christ. We do not perform these actions to draw attention to ourselves or out of obligation. We perform these actions to mount a spiritual marker as a testimony – a shirt from a Missions trip, a picture of a service project, a significant item that serves as a standard and testament of God's work in and through us. Let's place our own spiritual markers to guide future coaches and athletes, pointing them to the mighty, miraculous work of the Lord in, through and around us. Let's leave a mark that proclaims, *"As for me and my house, we will serve the Lord!"* ~Joshua 24:15

Questions

1. Do you have any markers that highlight your playing or coaching career?
2. Do you have spiritual markers that mark your journey with Christ?
3. What markers are you leaving behind for other Christians who are following your path?

Further Reading

Exodus 12:1-30; Psalm 78:1-12
Luke 22:14-22

Notes

31.

TAKE THE NEXT STEP

Now on the day that the tabernacle was raised up, the cloud covered the tabernacle, the tent of the Testimony; from evening until morning it was above the tabernacle like the appearance of fire…
Whenever the cloud was taken up from above the tabernacle, after that the children of Israel would journey; and in the place where the cloud settled, there the children of Israel would pitch their tents. At the command of the Lord the children of Israel would journey, and at the command of the Lord they would camp; as long as the cloud stayed above the tabernacle they remained encamped.
Numbers 9:15, 17-18

Successful athletic teams and successful businesses generally have similar values that guide their cultures. One such value highlights the process. Phrases such as "one day at a time," "baby steps,"and "take the next step" have been repeated so often, one cannot find a source to which we can attribute these phrases.

I found myself repeating these phrases again and again as I recovered from a pretty tough battle with the coronavirus in October 2020. I feel blessed that God started my healing process the morning I was considering going to the emergency room for breathing issues. I spoke with my physician that morning first. We discussed options and decided to try the plan that worked for my older brother earlier that summer before we would commit to a hospital trip. She promptly ordered the combination of home medical treatments which brought immediate positive results and started me on the road to recovery (Our God is on time, all the time!).

As an administrator and coach who was in the midst of our practice season at the time, it was impossible for me to bounce right back into normal activity. I tried several times to make brief appearances after three weeks at home, only to find myself exhausted, coughing and short of breath after each short stint with my students. An outbreak on campus forced the college to switch to remote learning in mid-November, which allowed me to recuperate at home through Christmas. Each day and week through this difficult journey I would review the steps forward I had taken, learn from mistakes, and ask myself what was an appropriate next step in my recovery. The phrase "baby steps" has entirely new meanings to me as I write, three months removed from my initial bout with the virus!

I originally had a different devotion to complete this 31-day journey. However, my recovery brought my own journey into sharp focus. As you close your journey with this book, I ask you the same question I asked myself every day as we ended 2020: What is your next step?

The Israelites found themselves facing a similar question after they crossed the Red Sea. Numbers 9 describes for us this time of uncertainty. Following the anniversary of the first Passover, verses 15-23 explain how God guided this nation of refugees.

We are told the tabernacle was raised and the cloud of the Lord covered the tent. During the day, it appeared as a cloud, but by night it appeared as fire. If the cloud moved from the tent, the refugees would follow the cloud until it settled. They would sojourn as long as the cloud remained in that location, whether it was two days, a month, or a year (v. 22).

"At the command of the Lord they remained encamped, and at the

command of the Lord they journeyed;"
~ Numbers 9:23

Two important points about this particular passage cannot be overlooked:

1. God's **presence** was **always with His people.** Jesus promised us in Matthew 28:20, *"and lo, I am with you always, even to the end of the age."* As you seek to move forward in your journey, know that Christ walks with you.

2. God provided the Israelites the **next step in the journey.** I am sure it was difficult at times for the sojourners, who longed for a land of their own. God had already promised He was taking them to such a land. He did not lay out a golden map for them. If you consider the fallen nature of man, that could have set them up for failure. They might have taken the map and set out on their own with all the steps laid out for them. In that scenario, I am certain pride would have overtaken them. No, instead, God required that they rely daily on Him. The beauty that is often overlooked in reading about the Exodus is that regardless of the uncertainty of the people and their repeated failures, God was faithful to His covenant with them and provided for their next step. Whether it was a movement of the cloud, or providing daily manna which was only good that day, God met their needs.

As you continue your faith journey, ask God to provide the next step for you, and be faithful to take that step. Your next step will likely be different than those around you. It may be taking a step to set up daily reading, or to meditate and delve more deeply into one particular passage or book. Your step may be to release a hidden burden, to break a pattern of sin, to heal a relationship, or to begin to fellowship with a local church. Whatever it is, I encourage you to take the next step. God is with you and will never leave you. If you fix your eyes on Him, He will order your steps for you, one step at a time.

Questions

1. What phrases have inspired you to embrace the process in your sport or job?
2. What steps did you take in order to embrace the process?
3. What next step do you sense God preparing for you?

Further Reading
Psalm 37:23; 119:105
Isaiah 30:21; James 4:13-16

Notes

ABOUT THE AUTHOR

Author Leo R. Sayles has impacted numerous athletes across the nation during his 34-year coaching career. Since 2007, his devotions, seminars, and workshops have inspired coaches of all levels as well.

In his 25+ years as a teacher, speaker, and former youth pastor, Sayles has combined sports analogies and stories to highlight scriptural truths and teaching.

Sayles has successfully coached sports at the middle school, high school, NAIA, NCAA Division 1 and Division 3 levels throughout his career.

A three-sport athlete in high school, Sayles was an All-Conference performer in the 400M and 4x100 relay at the University of La Verne.

Sayles currently works at Grove City College in Pennsylvania, where he serves as the Associate Athletic Director for Grove City's GEAR Sports Ministry and as Head Women's Volleyball Coach.

He and his wife, Tanya, have been married for over 30 years and have 6 grown children.

For more information about Coach Sayles, be sure to check out his website:
www.LeoSayles.com.

Find Coach Sayles on Social Media:

@LeoSayles

If you enjoyed Ordering Our Steps Book 2, be sure to go to Amazon.com and submit a review! Submit a star rating, and if you have a moment, add a written review.

ORDERING OUR STEPS

~ TO BE CONTINUED….

www.ingramcontent.com/pod-product-compliance
Lightning Source LLC
Chambersburg PA
CBHW061828040426
42447CB00012B/2863